JOÃO C. G. LOPES
NILTON FORMIGA

Is there a debt personality?

JOÃO C. G. LOPES
NILTON FORMIGA

Is there a debt personality?

The impacts of impulsiveness in the attitude to indebtedness on people who have compromised income due to consumption

ScienciaScripts

Publisher:
Sciencia Scripts
is a trademark of
International Book Market Service Ltd., member of OmniScriptum Publishing Group
17 Meldrum Street, Beau Bassin 71504, Mauritius
Printed at: see last page
ISBN: 978-620-0-93110-8

DEDICATORY

I dedicate this work to the love of my life, my girlfriend Jéssica Helena Maruoka da Silva, a companion who always motivated me, being responsible for my maturation as a person and a professional.

I also dedicate myself to my relatives and friends who have always been with me. I especially thank Iracema dos Santos Lopes, Isabela Orrico Gadelha do Espírito Santo and Victor Carvalho de Assis for all the support I found in moments of distress.

SUMMARY

4

1 INTRODUCTION

The process of purchasing decision making is studied under a number of theoretical frameworks, for example: Robert Hall and Marc Lieberman, in their book "Macroeconomics: Principles and Applications", who highlighted economic theory as a functional process of rationality, which aimed to assess the development and economic applicability with maximum welfare and utility in the process of negotiation in people's lives. However, in practice there are difficulties about the rationality at the time of purchase, an aspect that draws attention due to the incompatibility between need, planning and execution in the acquisition process (Gutierrez, 2004).

In general, the purchase is a process of deliberation, decision and action in the acquisition of a product or service. Thus, if there are several acquisitions or an acquisition greater than the person can pay, the individual will be in debt. For Marques and Friar (2003), indebtedness can be understood as the balance due to a third party (person, bank or any other institution relative to credit), with difficulty or economic limitation in repaying this balance, and then contracting a debt. This, in turn, is associated with factors such as: lack of planning, unemployment, diseases, bad faith, lower social classes, among others (Claudino, Nunes, Oliveira, & Campos, 2009).

Still in the sociodemographic sphere, indebtedness would have a relationship between social variables and financial literacy; a skill that helps in assertive and efficient decision making in the monetary scenario, interrupting the flow of indebtedness. This ability contemplates three constructs: Financial attitude, financial behavior and financial knowledge. Therefore, it can be seen that male individuals who do not have dependents and have higher levels of schooling and of own and family income present higher degrees of financial literacy, thus presenting a behavior of economic protection. In this sense, more than half of the population would have low levels of financial literacy (cf. Donadio, Campanario & Ranel, 2012; Lopes, Badio, Coimbra, Pozzan & Biazoto, 2014; Potrich, 2014; Potrich, Vieira & Kirch, 2015; Bahovec, Barbic & Palic, 2015; Jobim & Losekann, 2015).

Figure 1: Representation of the factors that influence indebtedness

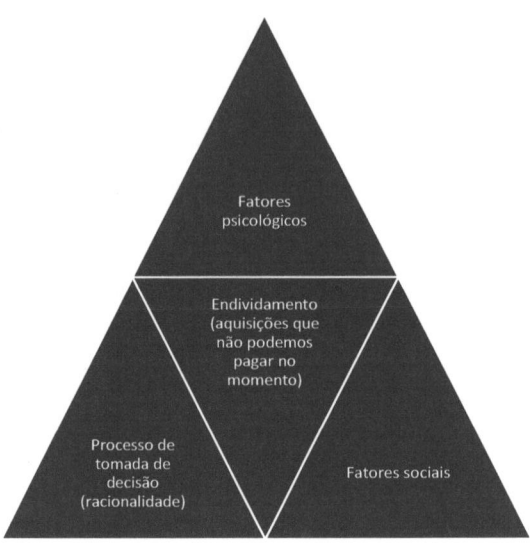

However, it should be emphasized that the above-mentioned variables are not the only ones responsible for the question of indebtedness; others, focusing on a more psychological perspective, could be explored, especially in what concerns personality traits, more, exclusively, impulsiveness traits as a predictive factor of the attitude to indebtedness. Although I consider impulsivity, as a search for sensations, to be a response available to all, it may, depending on the organization and psychic structure of the person, be considered a problem (cf. Formiga, Aguiar & Omar, 2008; Formiga, Omar & Aguiar, 2010).

Excessive impulsivity is part of the mental disorder picture, as pointed out by the American Psychiatric Association (APA), (2014), through the *Diasnostic and Statistical Manual of Mental Disorder* - DSM - which translated means, Diagnostic and *Statistical Manual* of Mental Disorders (DSM) (2014).

This manual establishes diagnostic criteria for mental disorders, based on consequences related to subjective suffering and impairment in social functioning (Dalgalarrondo, 2008; Silveira, Norton, Brandão & Roma-torres, 2011; Brandtner & Serralta, 2016). Some of these conditions present marked impulsiveness as clinical pictures of humor, personality and chemical dependence (Moeller, Barratt, Douherty, Schmitz & Swann, 2001).

Although impulsiveness is portrayed as a willingness to act quickly, unplanned and acquiring more consequences than benefits, as in psychiatric cases, being negative and destructive, some authors do not see it in full agreement, attributing positive functionality as in situations that require a restricted time for decision making, cases of athletes and high performance athletes (Gomes, 2016).

The studies proposed by Dickman (1990) reveal a connection between personality traits and cognitive function. The functional impulsiveness would be associated to the trait of enthusiasm, adventure and activity, compensating the amount of errors by the high production. Dysfunctional impulsivity, on the other hand, would be strongly related to ignoring concrete information. The first is associated with a low capacity to execute an activity in a thorough and systematic way, while the second implies the incapacity to operate in a slow and thorough way. Both impulsiveness are associated with boredom.

It should be noted that personality traits do not concern pathological issues, but the genetic dyad / environment would imply in the focus that the consistent individual characteristics of behavior, displayed by the individual in various situations, are usually conceived as arrangements, from which taxonomies are generated that allow the subject to express through behaviors, forms specific to himself and others when in social interaction (Formiga, Omar & Aguiar, 2010).

Studies on personality traits allowed Ernest Barratt to intensify the evaluation of this construct and to broaden the approach for evaluating impulsiveness. These authors developed a three-dimensional model, formed by "motor impulsivity", "impulsivity through non-planning" and "cognitive impulsivity" - Barratt Impulsivity *Scale* (BIS-11 - *Barratt Impulsiveness Scale*) (Barrat, 1983).

It is a self-filling scale consisting of 30 items associated with the manifestations of impulsiveness, based on the theoretical model proposed by Ernst Barrat. What determines a compulsive attitude towards purchases are external variables. Generally, people who present this behavior have the compulsive habit of using a credit card, for example. In this sense, from the perspective of Littwin (2008) who informs that the credit card promotes a greater participation of the lower and middle classes in the consumer environment.

In addition, there are also the intrinsic (internal) variables, characterized by impulsiveness, such as: urgency lack of perseverance and lack of premeditation. Studies show that among the aforementioned variables, urgency was the only one that acted as a predictor (Billieux et al., 2008; Velvet of the olive tree, Ikeda & Santos, 2004); this one is characterized by the high degree of immediacy and difficulty to resist the desire. Thus, the purchase of unnecessary objects and services is emphasized, increasing the post-purchase repentance in wage earners, male and low-income (Saleh, 2012).

In the face of such causalistic variables, it can be observed that psychological variables have been a very important space to understand the reasons that lead to the problem of indebtedness; thus, personality traits could probably be presented as one of the explanatory variables of the indebtedness phenomenon (Formiga, Omar & Aguiar, 2010).

Under this assumption, impulsivity is a variable that characterizes the hypothetical basis of this study, and is associated with indebtedness. This in turn can generate several losses, among them are: the shake in family structure, crises in relationships, depression, anxiety, shame, stress, feeling of powerlessness, guilt, humiliation, anguish, panic, discouragement, risks in disregarding previous debts, exaggeration in long-term consumption, increased amount of debt and disaster in personal finance and default (Hennigen, 2012; Artifon & Piva, 2013; SPC, 2015).

Figure 2: Representation of the psychological factors that influence indebtedness

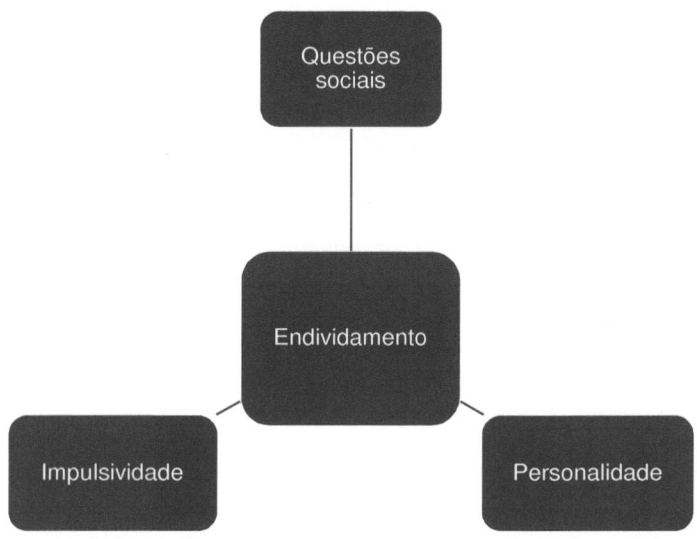

In view of this, indebtedness, within the thematic approach of this study, is therefore one of the major consequences of poor financial management. Therefore, the importance of investigating the correlation between impulsiveness and attitude towards indebtedness in adult population subjects is justified as the focus of this research.

Thus, new studies may be developed in order to find strategies that can deal with the attitudes of indebtedness in order to promote a better quality of life for the population and its better insertion in the social context, through the rescue of its self-assertion, also enabling greater financial control.

Therefore, the importance of studying the economically active public in order to prevent problems related to consumption is emphasized. Based on these premises and on the hypothetical basis mentioned above, this study generally aimed to verify the correlation between impulsiveness and attitude to indebtedness in adult population subjects.

2 THEORETICAL REFERENCE

2.1 INDEBTEDNESS AND VARIABLES THAT INFLUENCE PURCHASING ATTITUDE

Indebtedness is a recurrent theme on the national scene and given the relevance of the subject, it is considered to be of utmost importance that it be addressed and discussed. For Ribeiro (2018), the phenomenon is growing in Brazil and on one hand it is suggested that this result is due to the expansive supply of credit for individuals.

Campara, Vieira and Ceretta (2016, p. 7), explain that "the dissemination and ease of access to credit have, on the one hand, helped the lives of people, who now have a wide variety of resource options, but on the other, stimulates unconscious consumption.

Ribeiro (2018) adds that the main factor to blame for the distorted relationship with finances is the attitude of the debtor himself, due to his lack of subjective guidance regarding the financial assets offered to him.

Acordi (2019) disagrees stating that indebtedness does not have only its negative side. From the author's point of view, in some situations debts can bring benefits. There are also situations in which "controlled" indebtedness promotes a better quality of life for the individual. An example is a student who also has the need to work. Such an individual needs a vehicle to get from work to university. The solution for him will be a faster locomotion from one point to another, so, when getting into debt to solve this situation would be something advantageous.

Still according to the author, the same can occur with a person who will live in another region and there needs to acquire durable and essential goods such as stove, bed and refrigerator. By contracting debts to meet these needs, the individual satisfies their desire and interest, an aspect that promotes well-being and contributes to the quality of life. In short, under some conditions, a "controlled" debt can be advantageous and promotes an improvement in the quality of life (Acordi, 2019).

For Campara, Vieira and Ceretta (2016) the debt also occurs in situations considered positive, not only as a need to purchase, but as an opportunity. Having a clean name and belonging to the list of good payers is also a form of incentive to incur new debts, and if there is no discipline in the purchasing attitude the situation reverses, generating a negative connotation.

That said, it is important to emphasize the definition of an indebted person, which according to the Credit Protection Service (SPC), a person is considered indebted when he/she has installments of purchases due and/or loans. Thus, 20.2% of the population, the equivalent of 01 in every 05 people, fits this definition (SPC, 2015).

According to the National Consumer Debt and Default Survey (PEIC), when evaluating the risks of credit supply it was found that the average percentage of indebted families, with late payments of predated check, credit card, store card, personal loan, car payments and insurance, decreased from 61.6% in January 2016 to 55.6% in January 2017. However, the percentage for the same period, for the variable represented by those who claim not to be able to pay, increased from 9.0 to 9.3% (PEIC, 2017).

According to the results of a survey conducted in December 2018, in Brazil alone, more than 59% of Brazilian families had some type of debt, so that at least 23% of them said they had some sort of account in arrears, and 9% of these people guarantee that they cannot afford to pay their bills (Souza, 2019).

Artifon and Piva (2013) postulate that it is important to understand the psychological effects of indebtedness, considering that there is the occurrence of anxiety level of indebted people, so that their expectations for the future are impacted. Moreover, debt interferes with the quality of life and their styles. In this sense, it is evident in the behavior of the indebted subject the low self-esteem and the feeling of guilt.

Hennigen (2012) presents the negative impact on the life and the psychological of the indebted subject, so that basically the fact of being in debt or super indebted incurs a "burden of debt," so that to be in debt is to carry the burden of guilt, of impotence, of insomnia, of going through the privation of many things. Moreover, the burden of debt impedes the freedom of leisure and there is also the embarrassment of having to face suspicions and reproaches, so that all this represents a particularity of the one who sees himself as debtor.

Studies conducted by Souza (2019, p. 32) sought to identify the relationship "between situations of indebtedness, the individual's perception of their quality of life and health and symptoms of anxiety and depression. The results revealed that there is already several evidence in the literature of psychosomatic symptoms resulting from financial disorders and leading to stress in the individual. Symptoms such as depression, anxiety, low quality of life and in some cases, when the presence of extreme psychological pressure can result in suicide. In summary, the findings revealed that people with less indebtedness have a lower level of anxiety and a propensity to depression, as well as a better quality of life. The opposite is also confirmed.

Based on the opinion of France (2019), the field of behavioural finance reveals that psychological aspects, lived experiences and beliefs often influence the purchasing behaviour of individuals. Therefore, through the development of the Prospectus Theory it was possible to describe such influences and also to understand the biases that impact the rationality of purchasing decisions, effects and heuristics. On commemorative dates, for example, there is the highest probability of consumption related to gifts, which may or may not affect the debt process.

For Costa (2019), the decision-making process of consumption encompasses beyond personal interests, some individual peculiarities, psychological factors and influences of the environment where he lives. Binotto (2014) highlights that as for the external factors the most influential of the purpose of purchase to purchase behavior are the physical environment, culture, social class and family. Thus, the physical environment exerts, on average, the greatest influence on the individual's purchasing behavior, that is, the equivalent of 80.4%.

The variables that contribute to indebtedness and their consequences are evident from the reality presented. In this sense, occupation, financial literacy, gender, level of schooling and purchase in an electronic environment are observed.

According to a study conducted by Campara, Vieira and Ceretta (2016) with a community in the Mesoregion of the Central West of Rio Grande do Sul, to analyze the factor related to income and influence on indebtedness, the results showed that the lower the income, the greater the attitude to indebtedness. This reality reveals the socioeconomic and financial condition of the country's low-income population.

In what concerns the main factors of influence are pointed out in the cultural determinant, the culture and subculture variables; in the social determinant, the family and reference groups variables are found; in the personal determinant, the personality, the question of age, life cycle, economic conditions and occupation. In the psychological determinant, the variables related to beliefs, learning, attitudes, motivations and perception can be identified (Giareta, 2011).

Some results in research on the subject of financial education have shown that public servants, although they have credit facilities, are low-indebted so that people with high levels of attitude to indebtedness have low levels of financial education (Claudino, Nunes, Oliveira & Campos, 2009; Vieira, Flores & Coronel, 2013; Pacheco, Campara & Costa, 2017).

Still in relation to financial education, Lima (2016) adds that the area of the course attended by the individual influences the increase in the level of knowledge. Silva, Santos, Costa and Moreira (2016), conclude that students of accounting sciences have an average financial level and protect themselves so as not to incur debts.

It is suggested that indebtedness is related not only to financial education, but also to other factors. Thus, Rizzotto, Guareschi, Zilli and Tartas (2016), based on the results of studies conducted with Brazilian women, state that the variables related to the increase and decrease of indebtedness are related to the following variables: materialism, concern, pleasure, and power, while low indebtedness is associated with financial control.

According to Vieira et al (2013), the perception and behavior of financial risk can also be considered a set of evaluation that contributes to explain the indebtedness; for these authors, the perception of high risk can influence age and income, whereas, in relation to high risk behavior, it would be associated with low schooling, non-dependent and young people.

Considering the occurrence of indebtedness due to the influence of the variable level of education or area of knowledge, a study developed by Dias, Arenas e Silva (2017) with university students of Business Administration, Accounting and Economic Sciences identified the existence of finance subjects during the course and the investment profile of these academics is conservative. There is also a perceptual and real difference, so that university students do not consider themselves indebted, although there is a commitment of income between 31% and 60%. From the perspective of Littwin (2008), the credit card promotes a greater participation of the lower and middle classes in the consumer environment.

2.2 IMPULSIVITY AND ITS RELATION TO INDEBTEDNESS

Impulsivity is defined as a dynamic phenomenon. Traditionally, impulsivity has been seen as a temperamental characteristic, a hereditary element that in a certain period of time is stable and can also be a phenomenon related to some type of injury to the central nervous system. Abreu, Tavares and Cordás (2008),

It is therefore understood that the impulse is one of the major generators of debt. According to Abreu, Tavares and Cordás (2008), impulsiveness is conceptualized as a behavioral characteristic marked by rapid reactions in an unplanned manner, without any evaluation of the consequences. It can also be presented only in a partial way, with a preferential focus on immediate aspects to the detriment of future consequences.

Research related to impulse disorders has doubled in recent years and social vehicles flood society with potentially rewarding opportunities added to access to services, products and instant credit (Tavares, 2008).

Figueira and Pereira (2014) directly relates self-control and impulse buying, as well as the search for power and prestige through compulsive buying and anxiety. Such behaviors increase compulsions, adding the relationship between credit card attitude and consumer debt.

On the other hand, the results obtained by the studies of Siqueira et al., (2012) in relation to the amount of sales made through the Internet in Brazil that reach 14.8 billion reais, call attention. There is a great possibility of impulsive purchases through the Internet, through rational appeals such as: 24-hour stores, greater variety and lower prices than competitors, among others.

Reinforcing the statement made by the above-mentioned authors, the facilities of offers presented by the mass media and marketing develop in the individual the supposed need that is manifested by the desire to be and to have matter for capitalism. However, few are those who are prepared for the assimilation of so many offers and facilities, and as a consequence become indebted and in some cases defaulting people. Faced with this, indebtedness generates serious consequences for the individual and can lead to suicide (Lucena et al. , 2014).

2.3 IMPULSIVITY FROM A PSYCHOLOGICAL SCIENCE PERSPECTIVE: DEFINITION AND MEASURES

Impulsivity is implicit in human conduct, implying individual and collective effects. Before proceeding with the approach on such implications and effects, it is necessary to conceive that impulsivity presents numerous concepts.

Barratt and Patton (1983) consider the concept of impulsivity a relevant construct. Although it has been described as a negative or dysfunctional characteristic associated with various disorders, it is not always correlated only to negative consequences, and may therefore contribute to subjectivity (Gomes, Malloy-Diniz, Lage, Miranda, Paula, Costa & Albuquerque, 2017).

In biopsychosocial terms, impulsivity is a pattern of behaviour and not an isolated act. It refers to an action that happens suddenly, without the subject having the opportunity to think and analyze the consequences. Impulsivity almost always focuses on risks, but individuals are not interested in the results of these risks. For impulsive people, what interests them at the moment of impulsiveness is the search for sensation (Moeller, Barrattt, Dougherty, Schmitz, & Swann, 2001; Ribeiro 2013; Gattás, 2014).

Still according to the authors, under the social aspect, impulsiveness happens through a behavior that was acquired/learned in the family environment, a space where the child learns to present the immediate reaction to achieve what pleases him. In this sense, impulsive individuals do not analyze the consequences of their actions, either for themselves or for other people. Thus, "a definition that includes the social aspects of impulsiveness should incorporate the fact that impulsiveness often has an impact not only on the impulsive individual, but also on others".

For Vasconcelos (2012), one of the most used definitions in the literature suggests that impulsivity should be defined as a tendency to react in a fast and unplanned manner to internal or external stimuli without taking into account the negative consequences that these actions may cause on oneself or others.

The author also states that impulsiveness can be defined as a complex construct and it represents distinct cognitive and behavioral patterns characterized by decision making without taking into account long-term effects, difficulty in waiting for an event, difficulty in inhibiting overbearing responses and behaviors inappropriate to the context and also the search for sensations (cf. Vasconcelos, 2012).

According to Malloy-Diniz et al. (2010), impulsivity is a complex phenotype with distinct cognitive and behavioral patterns that generate immediate and medium or long-term dysfunctional consequences. For Arcer and Santisbetan (2006), impulsivity is the result of the interaction of independent characteristics, and can be functional or dysfunctional.

A concept that has been widely accepted is that impulsiveness occurs when: a) there is a change in the course of action without prior conscious judgment; b) unthinking behavior occurs or; c) a tendency to act with a lower level of planning compared to individuals with the same intellectual level is manifested (Moeller et al. 2001).

Moeller, et al., (2001) define impulsiveness as a predilection for quick responses without any planning and that happens through external or internal stimuli, in an inconsequential way, that is, the negative effects coming from the action that can reach the person himself or even other people are not considered. This definition frames impulsiveness as a pattern of behavior and not just an isolated or sporadic act, based on lack of planning, which implies not considering the risks in advance.

However, one of the authors who has been most dedicated to the study of impulsivity - Barratt (1959) described impulsivity as a complex personality trait related to a tendency to perform fast, unplanned and often inefficient and inadequate motor actions.

In parallel, other studies have also shown that motor impulsivity and unplanned impulsivity are highly related to "narrow" and dysfunctional impulsivity. An example is the research conducted by Whitside & Lynam, (2001). They identified that motor impulsivity often has higher correlation coefficients than unplanned impulsivity. On the other hand, cognitive impulsivity usually shows lower or non-significant relationships with impulsivity scales that are more related to lack of inhibition.

Still regarding the authors who researched impulsiveness, some of them are still cited as examples: Ferreira (2013) who, through a case study, sought to identify motor impulsivity; Parcias et al., (2014) who, based on an article published in the Health Care Journal, developed a thematic approach on impulsive behavior in university students. Another outstanding publication on the subject is Guerra et al., (2016), which made an analytical study of the relationships between personality traits, impulsive buying and compulsive buying.

In short, despite the conceptual difficulty, it is recognized that there is a propensity for quick and unplanned reactions from internal or external stimuli, annulling the negative consequences resulting from the actions that determine impulsiveness.

2.4 COGNITIVE BEHAVIOURAL PATTERNS - DISORDERS AND OTHER FACTORS ASSOCIATED WITH IMPULSIVITY

In the Diagnostic and Statistical Manual of Mental Disorders - DSM 5th Edition or DSM-V, impulsivity-related disorders have a separate chapter, however, anxiety, personality type and mood may be associated with increased impulsivity. Although described in the manual, the establishment of a term to characterize impulsivity is still studied. (Araujo, Malloy-Diniz & Rocha, 2009).

When it comes to personality, Rocha (2013) describes several attempts to formulate a concept for this term from various nuances. However, some common terms are presented such as emotions, thoughts, behaviors, the environmental context and stability in time. From Beck and Alford's (2000) point of view, personality is understood as the sum of actions, cognitive processing, emotional reactions, needs that operate in and are influenced by the environment.

For Araujo, Malloy-Diniz & Rocha (2009) there is a relationship between impulsiveness and personality traits - a fluid term in psychology, however, it will depend on the theoretical side used. Thus, even in situations where impulsivity is not associated with the symptomatic picture of a disorder, a greater expression of this phenotypic trait can lead to significant damage, for example, there is evidence of the relationship between impulsivity and risk behavior in traffic.

Regarding development periods, according to Otto, Willhelm and Almeida (2016), there is a correlation between intelligence and impulsiveness. These authors developed research with adolescents who had higher scores on impulsiveness. Results presented lower scores on intelligence tasks. However, there is no way to state that one variable inhibits the other, but the interference of one on the other.

Although there are differences of opinion about the number of factors that make up impulsiveness, there is a consensus about its multidimensional nature. In an informal way, impulsivity manifests itself, among other ways: impatience, negligence, extroversion, involvement in risky situations, underestimated notion of harm and search for novelties, sensations and pleasure. These factors can also appear as symptoms of multiple psychiatric disorders (Moraes, 2011). In this sense, there is a growing number of investigations that seek to understand the role of impulsiveness in psychiatric disorders.

Table 1, below, presents the survey carried out in the researches dealing with impulsiveness and its relationship with psychiatric disorders, gender, age, behavior and other factors related to conduct, ethnic-social patterns, among others, with their respective researchers and year of publication.

Picture: Factors associated with impulsivity

Impulsivity and Psychiatric Disorders	Author/Searcher - year
Attention deficit and hyperactivity disorder	Malloy-Diniz, Fuentes, Leite, Correa, & Bechara, 2007.
Antisocial personality disorder	Swann, Lijffijt, Lane, Steinberg, & Moeller, 2009b.
Bipolar Mood Disorder	Swann, Lijffijt, Lane, Steinberg, & Moeller, 2009a.
Borderline personality disorder	Matioli, Matheus Rozário, Rovani, Érica Aparecida, Noce, Mariana Araújo 2014.
Conduct disorder	Gao,Chen, Jia, Ming, &Yao, 2016
Psychopathology	Malloy-Diniz et al.,2010)
Prefrontal injuries and executive functions	e.g. Cohen, Rosenbaum, Kane, Warnken& Benjamin, 1999; Brower & Price, 2001; Hoaken, Shaughnessy & Pihl, 2003; Chen & Vazsonyi, 2011)
Risk behavior in traffic	Loo, 1978, 1979; Eric, 2005; Araujo, Malloy-Diniz & Rocha, 2009),
Suicidal behavior	Malloy-Diniz, Neves, Abrantes, Fuentes & Corrêa, 2009).
Tobacco consumption	(e.g. Mitchell, 1999),
Alcohol consumption	(e.g. Echeburúa, Bravo& Aizpiri, 2008; MacDonald, Erickson, Wells, Hathaway& Pakula, 2008),
Abuse and dependence on substance	Salgado, Malloy-Diniz, Campos, Abrantes, Fuentes, Bechara & Corrêa, 2009.
Age	e.g. Eysenck, Pearson, Easting & Allsopp, 1985; Claes, Vertommen & Braspenning, 2000),
Gender	E.G. Eysenck et al., 1985; Luengo et al., 1991; Claes et al., 2000; Struber, Luck & Roth, 2008),
Schooling	E.G. Claes et al., 2000),

Source: Adapted by the author.

In view of the above, it is clear that there is a multiplicity of factors related to impulsiveness. In addition to the factors mentioned above, others presented by Vasconcelos (2012) are also mentioned. The author reveals that impulsivity can be associated with a large number of unadaptative human behaviors such as sexual risk behavior, domestic violence and smoking.

2.5 CONTEMPORARY CONSUMPTION: A CONTEXTUALIZATION WITH AN INDIVIDUALIST FOCUS

First of all, it is important to highlight that consumption and consumerism do not present the same definition. Consumption is understood as the practice that leads the individual to acquire something that is in accordance with his/her need and/or survival. Consumerism, on the other hand, defines the act of acquiring a product that in reality is not really needed by the person who purchases it (Lago & Reis, 2016).

For Marchesini (2012, p. 14), in post-modernity "the aestheticisation of everyday life and the triumph of signs portray the subordination of production to consumption in the form of marketing, with an increasing rise in the concept of product, design and advertising".

And it is this supposed rise that the media uses to persuade the human being among so many other persuasive strategies. People are conditioned to think that what is important in today's society is that everyone consumes, since man becomes valued for the objects he possesses, for his financial conditions and the ability to acquire, not only for his labor, as it was before, in the society of producers (Pólon, 2011).

The author also reports that in some way, individuals seek to consume. People with greater purchasing power are easier to do so, however, those in the poorest section of the population find it more difficult to consume, which often leads to the search for alternative means that are unfeasible and illegal to conquer the much dreamed of product. This fact is associated with the great number of thefts and violent acts that take place so that it is possible to achieve what one wants without analyzing the limits and consequences of these acts.

Caron, Lefreve and Lefreve (2015) state that in the current social scenario, what defines someone is the way they consume, that is, the individual is qualified by what he or she consumes, just as identities are also produced through consumption. In this sense, differences in market access represent social inequalities.

For Pólon (2011), in its essence consumption encompasses society as a whole, however the way consumption occurs classifies the individual in a given group, so consumption is not just something done out of necessity, but an element of social selection. In this respect, it is the characteristic of the product and the quantity acquired that determines to which class the individual belongs.

We are part of a society that values what you have more than what you really are. Personal objects, what the individual wears and the technological equipment he possesses, profile presented in social networks define the consumer in contemporary society, that is, the society of consumers. (Lago & Reis, 2016).

Marchesini (2012) asserts that many times, a person searches for a certain product only in order to fit into a group or tribe, or only as an ostentatious artifact that imposes a certain power over the other person. Therefore, in this case, social alienation is characterized as one of the most perverse conditions imposed on society in recent decades.

To be included in today's society, man must be a consumer. This leads us to believe that consumption is not only the result of production, but also, in the figurative sense, the passport to social inclusion. The individual is included in society according to the product he or she consumes. Consumption relations happen quickly and the individual needs to adapt to the imposed pace, otherwise he will be excluded from the group (Pólon, 2011).

The trend today is simply to buy. Even having a product that still meets the needs of the individual, when faced with a new one, he chooses the novelty. There are several factors that lead to this type of attitude: the need to keep up with today's trends means that the person is always consuming, since if they do not keep up with the most modern trends, they end up being labeled as outdated. Another persuasive way that leads to consumption are the advertisements (Lago & Reis, 2016).

According to Pólon (2011, p.12), the human being has always gone in search of the best things in order not to become old-fashioned. For the author, "no matter how many things we have, there will always be new things being launched to the market, and in a consumer society who does not update himself, is rejected. In this sense, the individual stops consuming of his own free will, and begins to consume in a forced manner so that he feels included.

As if it were not enough for the medium to be influenced by consumption choices, the consumer himself is also shaped according to what he decides to consume. The way one consumes and what one consumes determines one's status and one sees oneself inserted in a specific social group. What is consumed in the consumer society is decisive for the identity of the individual. What he buys determines who he is (Pólon, 2011).

In order to add more and more for consumption, the market is based on various artifacts, such as advertisements, advertising, and promotions (Lago & Reis, 2016). Thus, "Acting ideologically on society, advertising creates ever more uniform consumer needs, and gradually annuls cultural differences" (Sposito, p. 64).

One way to encourage consumption is television advertising. This is the purpose of this type of service and it is highly appreciated by its target audience: the consumer. In this sense, TV has been configured as a privileged space that tunes in to all market trends and the fashion scene in contemporary society where consumption gives rise to social production of identity and social insertion (Caron, Lefreve & Lefreve, 2015, p. 3).

Lago e Reis (2016) postulate that for consumption to develop, people are led to buy immediately, causing them to have a pseudo-happiness. However, when people are forced to live with the fact that they have to discard things, "with the novelty and the prospects of instant obsolescence, the post-modern culture of consumption makes society unable to organize coherently for the future. (Marchesini, 2012, p. 15).

Marchesini (2012) warns that the most worrying thing is that concepts considered fundamental and of great importance are impacted by the capitalist forces from marketing and advertising. This causes sustainability, as a practical discourse, to be reduced to a simple argument that overvalues brands.

Different from what is aimed at, which is the attempt to alleviate the environmental partner mismatches throughout the productive life cycle. This includes the waste that is generated and discarded by this unbridled consumerism, a major aggravating factor in the consequences of poverty and environmental destruction (Marchesini, 2012).

It seems that consumption in the contemporary world is far from the primordial character of what originated it if we analyze the roots of this trend. In the history of consumption, there is an inclination towards development in a comprehensive way, with a view to moving the economy, as it is today, but also a means of reaching a mass population, different from excluding them or labeling them according to what one consumes.

In this sense, with a view to explaining the origin of consumption, it is stated in Pólon (2011, p. 1) that: "Among the various historical events and factors that led to the constitution of the current consumer society, one moment in history in particular deserves highlighting, the Industrial Revolution.

The author continues to state that the beginning of the advent occurred in England in the mid-18th century. This event consolidated the mechanized factory system, characterized by urban expansion, a revolution in the means of transportation, and the technology was developed, replacing the human labor force by the use of the machine.

Pólon (2011) also explains that the reason for the search for the use of the machine was the need to meet the market pressures, since the capitalists were looking for some way to produce the goods more intensively. Thus, as time went by, the machines were being perfected from the techniques that were increasingly evolving. Besides achieving greater agility, the industrial machines generated lower production costs. With this, it was possible that the products were marketed at lower costs leading to increased consumer demand.

Spósito (2000) asserts that the constituent process of mass consumption society promoted, from the 19th century onwards and specifically during the 20th century, homogenised cultural values under the sphere of capitalist rule. Such event was the result of the manufacturing industry that with the use of machines started to produce in large scale.

In this context, the society of consumers emerged, which focused on the person as consumer. In this context, there was the purpose that all products were developed in order to serve the consumer public, so that the production of various goods could serve as alternatives and options of choice, for the cheapest, the most beautiful, the most enjoyable, finally, the consumer had the opportunity to select. (Polon, 2011)

From the point of view of Zanirato and Rotondaro (2016), it was in modernity that the desire to consume more and more arose. So the desire to purchase occurred because people considered that through consumption they could obtain personal satisfaction. And it is for this reason that today's society is seen as the consumer society. Nevertheless, this capitalist process that encourages mass production, market advancement and intense commercial flow has generated alienation in people because they have to adapt to a system of media values (Marchesini, 2012).

Grando and Magro (2011) postulate that consumption in contemporaneity is a way to accelerate the economy and reaffirm capitalism as an economic system. In this direction, Lago and Reis (2016) emphasize the impossibility of disassociating consumption from capitalism, since these two elements are duly organized with a view to making a profit.

On the other hand, the issue is contradictory when analyzed in the context of solidarity economy, because as explained by Zanirato and Rotondaro (2016), consumption has generated major ecological problems, which leads to the search for solutions to these problems, characterizing a constant conflict between consumption and environmental protection.

Pólon (2011) mentions the satisfactory character of consumption. For the author, what the consumer society wants is to have the possession of the products that are available and with this, accumulate as many goods as possible. So that the best products are always more in demand, since there is the impression that they are capable of satisfying needs and providing the desired happiness.

2.5.1 CONSUMERISM DUE TO IMPULSIVENESS AND LACK OF REFLECTION

In order to present a theoretical basis for the study of impulse buying, impulsiveness will be understood as the absence of reflection between a stimulus (provided, for example, by the environment in which the subject is inserted) and the response of the individual (Bonomo, Mainardes & Laurett, 2017).

Studies carried out in the field of psychology on impulsiveness affirm that this phenomenon is linked to the behavioral dimension of the human personality, being represented, as previously explained by other authors, as being the immediate response to an environmental stimulus, making people totally reactive to circumstances. In this sense, self-control, as a complex phenomenon could be relevant to meet these behaviors (Hanna & Todorov, 2002).

In Barratt's model, motor impulsivity suggests the non-inhibition of context-incoherent responses (Malloy-Diniz, et al., 2010). This leads to the understanding that the absence of self-control leads to the identification of one of the components that conceive impulsivity as proposed by the model: Motor component.

2.6 LABORATORY MEASURES AND IMPULSIVITY ASSESSMENT TOOLS

Laboratory measures of impulsiveness have been developed by measuring their different components based on tasks where future planning skills, speed of response, errors made, skills to inhibit overpowering motor responses and ability to sustain focused attention to a specific task are evaluated (cf. Amato, Brunoni, & Boggio, 2018; Teixeira, 2014).

Impulsivity is commonly assessed through observation or reporting of behaviours and through the use of evaluative tools such as inventories and questionnaires. Quoted in this research, Eysenck's Impulsivity Inventory (Eysenck & Eysenck, 1977), the Self-Reporting Questionnaires that are generally associated with more stable personality traits, and the scores reflect people's own perception.

However, there are still more influential models in the understanding of impulsivity, for example, the Dickman model, impulsivity questionnaire studied by Gomes (2016) and that of Ernest Barratt - Barratt *Impulsiveness Scale*, proposed by Ernst Barratt, which is among the most prominent specific impulsivity measures (Barratt, 1959) proposed by Otto, Willhelm and Almeida (2016).

Impulsivity assessment from self-reported scales can be done by means of personality assessment instruments or specific impulsivity assessment measures. In the first group, indirect measures of impulsivity included in the NEO-PI-R (impulsivity facet of neuroticism and self-discipline facet of conscientiousness) (Costa & MacCrae, 1992) or the search for novelties present in the Clonninger's Inventory of Temperament and Character (Cloninger et al., 1993).

In the clinical context, evidence of validity can be maximized when variables are measured by different methods, particularly when they produce discrepant results. This evaluation contributes to collect data more broadly and facilitates the understanding of the forces and limitations of the individual in his daily life (Vasconcelos, 2012).

According to Vasconcelos, Sergeant, Corrêa, Mattos and Malloy-Diniz (2014), based on Dickman's thought, the subject, by presenting impulsiveness, generally, he adapts to a certain context, for which, he refers to a functional impulsiveness, being it, beneficial. But when the impulsivity is not adequate to a certain context, a dysfunctional impulsivity occurs, which is presented under difficulties or with characteristics of pathological traits, leading to negative consequences (cf. Claes et. al., 2000).

Thus, Dickman (1990), suggests that the construction and measurement of impusiveness is organized in two dimensions-domains: on the one hand, there is a dysfunctional impusiveness, which can be attributed to the tendency of the personnel to act with less reflection when a problem or situation requires it; on the other hand, there is the functional impulsiveness, which is associated with the tendency to act without thinking or precipitate, especially when behavior is favorable to action. This construct can still be expressed in various ways, ranging from the inability to plan for the future, with the favoring of choices that provide immediate satisfaction and without pondering the consequences for oneself and others, to the occurrence of violent or aggressive behavior (cf. Del-Bem, 2005; Gomes, 2016).

But, in the conception of the above-mentioned authors, it is possible to state that such consequences do not present themselves as negative impulsive behaviour. According to Claes et. al. (2000), when evaluating the studies that relate impulsivity and cognitive functions, it is observed that, in the experimental task of the studies, those subjects that present high impulsivity, manfist responses faster, with positive results with low error.

According to the above-mentioned authors, they observed that when a sufficiently short one is presented for the respondents to make a decision, the subjects characterized as very impulsive are more precise in their decisions than those with a low level of impulsiveness.

2.6.1 IMPULSIVITY IN THE MODEL PROPOSED BY DICKMAN - DICKMAN'S IMPULSIVITY INVENTORY (DII).

Impulsivity almost always brings serious harm to the person. In this sense, Dickman (1990) presents a dichotomous definition of this phenomenon; from the development of an instrument of self-report, created in the year 1990, called: *Dickman's Impulsivity Inventory (DII)*, also known by its simple abbreviated form: Dickman's Model, aiming to perform an investigation of the impulsivity construct, through the dimensions: functional and dysfunctional. Through this instrument, impulsivity is investigated through its components, leading, therefore, to instigate several researchers and scholars of the subject to use this instrument in their investigations.

From his research, Dickman can conclude that impulsiveness is not always associated with negative consequences. Thus, in his proposed model, impulsivity has a connection with cognitive and personality functioning, having a functional and dysfunctional side. By responding impulsively the individual tends to act with reduced attention, but in an appropriate manner based on a certain event (Dickman, 1990).

In this sense, functional impulsivity is revealed, since this type of impulsivity is considered beneficial. However, when the response is given impulsively and without adequacy to a given context, it reveals a characteristic behaviour of dysfunctional impulsivity and is then characterized as a difficulty. In this type of impulsiveness the individual tends to act with less reflection when required by a problem or situation. However, if one considers the phenomenon of psychopathology, impulsivity is a personality trait (Dickman, 1990).

Thus, Dickman also states that in very simple situations the consequences of impulsiveness are not always considered negative. This will only occur in a situation where a rapid response can be issued with few errors and also when the time available to make a decision, or to carry out a certain action or movement, is restricted. In these two cases, it is suggested that impulsivity seems to have a positive consequence.

Dickman and Meyer (1998) in their study found that high impulses are more accurate than low impulses, when individuals need to process information extremely quickly, presenting problems for the model of compensation between velocity and precision.

Given the importance of the Dickman Model, the Dickman Impulsivity Inventory (DII; Dickman, 1990) is presented, consisting of 23 items divided into two sub-scales: 11 IF and 12 ID measures. The answers are either affirmative or negative. Gomes et al., (2017) stress that the Dickman Impulsivity Inventory (Dickman, 1990) consists of 23 self-reported items, of which 11 were designed to measure functional impulsivity and 12 to measure dysfunctional impulsivity. In its first version, the format created by Dickman presented a dichotomous response model, that is, (false or true)

In Gomes' (2016) theoretical approach, the Dickman model, as can be observed above, first emerged from the investigation of an instrument of self-reporting in order to distinguish dysfunctional impulsivity and functional impulsivity.

For this purpose, the author created a questionnaire presenting 63 items, so that most of them, i.e. 23 items refer to dysfunctional impulsivity and the minority, the equivalent of 17 refer to functional impulsivity. According to the results of studies, "values of internal consistency equal to 0.83 (Cronbach's alpha) for the functional dimension and 0.86 (Cronbach's alpha) for the dysfunctional dimension" are shown. Gomes (2016, p.13).

 The author also reports that the two dimensions have a tendency to think less in time before the action. It has been observed, therefore, that functional impulsivity is not a behavior completely alien to cognition, since the individual acts in a rational way. In this case, a quick way of deciding and acting occurs, which brings benefits to the one who practices the action and to the situation by which he was driven.

Dickman (2000) reveals that in individuals with a greater tendency to impulsiveness there is a deficit of attentional focus and this happens easily. However, those with less impulsive behavior change the focus of attention less easily.

Therefore, the individuals who show themselves with greater intensity of impulses are inconsequential, that is, they do not think before acting, since during this time they would be thinking about how to carry out such an act they would have difficulty to be aware of the decision that would be made.

The same goes for less impulsive people. The tendency is that such people may be hampered in the execution of activities that require a quick change in focus because their attention is fixed on their initial motivation.

Dickamn (1990) postulates that impulsivity is an orientation to act in an inconsequent way to the acts that are performed by a certain individual and this happens with most people who have the same intellectual potential. In other terms, functional impulsivity represents a personality trait that allows the individual to process information quickly. Dysfunctional impulsivity refers to the agile way of doing things and in this fast way of doing things, mistakes occur because the individual has difficulty acting and making decisions at the same time.

Still on the dimensions of impulsiveness, Dickman (1990) describes Functional Impulsiveness as a way to respond quickly, but in an appropriate way, suggesting through the response an expressive and spontaneous form that denotes much more an ability to act and act immediately, so that the consequences arising from this behavior bring greater pleasure and satisfaction due to the feeling of achievement. The opposite happens when dysfunctional impulsiveness enters the scene. With this behavior the individual makes mistakes, deceits and furthermore the consequences become great losses that can bring other consequences to the individual who has committed such acts.

Dickman (1990) explains that there is a close correlation between the two dimensions: functional and dysfunctional, being therefore associated with distinct personalities. Dickman also asserts that both dimensions tend to have unthinking attitudes when compared to most people of equal capacity. However, people with a high functional impulsiveness generate positive consequences, but for people with a higher load of dysfunctional impulsiveness they can be put in difficulties by themselves.

Several authors point out in the literature the feasibility of the self-reporting instrument proposed by Dickman to investigate the impulsivity construct. In this sense, Fernandes (2014) emphasizes the evaluation of the functional and dysfunctional aspect proposed by Dickman (1990) that occurred through the conception of Dickman's Impulsivity Inventory (DII). According to the author, this instrument has presented accuracy rates of $\alpha = 0.74$ for dysfunctional impulsivity and $\alpha = 0.85$ for functional impulsivity (Fernandes, 2014).

As Gomes et al (2017) states, Dickman's (1990) impulsivity scales are classified in two dimensions: functional impulsivity - occurs when most of the time the individual is able to put his thoughts into words quickly. Dysfunctional impulsivity occurs when the individual often does not spend time thinking about a situation before acting.

Gomes et al., (2017) developed a research aiming to validate, translate and adapt *Dickman's Impulsivity Inventory (DII)* instrument in order to apply it to adult people in Brazil in order to analyze the feasibility of its application in Brazilian research. The thematic cutout for the study was due to the fact that this model is the only impulsivity instrument capable of investigating Functional Impulsivity (IF) and Dysfunctional Impulsivity (ID).

Thus, the above-mentioned authors decided to adopt an ordinal response scale containing five points, so that the individual could then choose between: I totally disagree, I disagree neutral, I agree and I totally agree. This type of questionnaire is called Likert, being therefore a tool that generates, but sensitivity.

For study purposes, the above-mentioned authors started first from the translation and adaptation stages. Through a rigorous methodology, the instrument was translated and adapted and in the meantime the two independent translations were included. The synthesis of the translations and the two backtranslations were done independently, and biases and discrepancies were also analysed by two specialists with experience in cross-cultural adaptation.

Continuing with the development of research, the final version was applied to 405 university students. Once the data were fully analyzed, through Confirmatory Factor Analysis (AFC) and Exploratory Factor Analysis (AFE), the convergent and divergent validity were also evaluated, with Pearson's correlative analyses.

Internally, consistency was assessed through Cronbach's Alpha (α). To check the test-retest reliability the Intraclass Correlation Coefficient (ICC) and the Student t-test were used. This was paired in order to compare the responses, considering the interval of two weeks (Gomes et al., 2017).

Following the development of the research, the authors interpreted the data by means of Exploratory Factorial Analysis (EFA). Convergent and divergent validity were assessed by performing Pearson's correlation analysis.

Internal consistency was evaluated using Cronbach's Alpha (α), and test-retest reliability was verified using the Intraclass Correlation Coefficient (ICC) and paired Student t-test to compare responses over a two-week interval. AFC indicated that the 23-item version did not match the model settings.

The AFE with 18 items indicated appropriate adjustment measures [CFI = 0.923; TLI = 0.90; and RMSEA = 0.057], which together with the values of internal consistency (IF = 0.73 and ID = 0.75), convergent and divergent validity and the retest, confirmed the quality of the instrument in the Brazilian version (Gomes et al., (2017)).

Confirmatory Factorial Analysis (AFC) indicated that the 23-item version did not suit the model settings; Exploratory Factorial Analysis (AFE) with 18 items indicated appropriate adjustment measures [CFI = 0.923; TLI = 0.90 and RMSEA - Root Mean Square Error of Approximation (RMSEA) - mean square root of approximation error = 0.057. The values of internal consistency (IF = 0.73 and ID = 0.75), convergent and divergent validity and the retest confirmed the quality of the instrument in the Brazilian version.

In summary, the studies by Gomes et al., (2017) pointed out that the Brazilian version of IBD presents adequate psychometric properties to be applied in Brazilian adults, or rather, after the evaluation of the psychometric properties of Br-DI, suggest that the adaptation of IBD is valid and reliable to be used in Brazilian research with adult individuals.

It is understood, therefore, that by bringing Dickman's (1990) theory to the subject of impulsivity and indebtedness, it can be seen that the individual who acts precipitately both in the purchasing attitude and in the decision-making process, reveals a behaviour of dysfunctional impulsivity. The practice of compulsive purchases is evident in his daily life and these are characterized by installment payments, excessive spending on credit cards, in short; debts and more debts.

Most of the time these individuals commit almost all their monthly income. There are also those who are in debt in such a way that all their monthly income is fully committed. Others spend more than they earn. The worst thing is that after all this, the individual finds himself immersed in real financial chaos, and from this consequence other consequences arise.

2.6.2 BARRATT IMPULSIVITY SCALE (BIS-11)

The study of impulsivity was given great dedication by the author Barratt (1959,1993). Regarding the studies already developed on the subject, Ferrari et al (2019), states that there are several scientific researches that have sought to understand the factors that influence individual decision making in different contexts.

Fernades (2014) referred to Ernest S. Barratt's (1993) model as one of the most important to explain impulsive behavior. Based on the instrument, the author emphasized it in her thesis, bringing to the literature a historical synthesis of the proposed model design.

Thus, the author reports that in the 60's, aiming at creating a questionnaire that could evaluate the characteristics that would influence the performance in psychomotor evaluation tests, Barratt idealized the impulsivity scale that is well known nowadays. The researcher's intention was to create his own scale for impulsivity. Thus, from the observation that determinant variables for the quality of test responses presented independent behavior when related to anxiety assessment scales.

Since then, Barratt has developed the BIS - Barratt Impulsiveness Scale, which has been officially reviewed more than 10 times in the period from 1965 to 1965 and 1995. The current version is BIS-11. In the last 3 decades, Barratt's concern has been specifically the structural improvement of the scale through factor analyses in order to identify its correlation with other impulsiveness models (Fernades, 2014).

Vasconcelos (2012) postulates that there is not yet a single consolidated theoretical instrument that can explain the behaviour. However, one finds in the literature the conception that the construct is revealed by a predisposition to an urgent and improvised reaction to internal or external stimuli, disregarding the negative consequences that such actions may bring both to the practitioner and to other individuals in the context.

In relation to the purchasing attitude, it appears in Barratt (1959) that in its scale of impulsiveness determines some affirmations related to the purchasing attitude: The habit of saving, that is, of saving regularly;

impulse purchases and the interest in installment purchases, even investing much more than the individual earns.

In this sense, the author identified impulsiveness as a complex personality trait associated with a propensity to perform rapid motor actions, which happen without planning and frequently, characterized by inefficiency and an incorrect way. Thus, the author conceived in 1959 the *Impulsivity Scale (BIS),* which until reaching the current version it has gone through several previous versions. The initial version of the scale aimed to associate impulsivity with psychomotor efficiency and anxiety. After deepening studies on the subject, Barratt developed other versions, for example, the version BIS-10 (Ávila-Batista & Rueda 2011).

The Barratt Scale of Impulsivity (BIS-11) is one of the most widely used instruments, although other assessment tools are considered to exist in this area. The *Barratt impulsiveness scale - BIS 11* was specifically designed to evaluate the behavior of the impulsivity construct as a personality feature. The scale was designed to create an instrument that could discriminate against impulsivity and other behaviors, such as the search for sensation, extroversion, and the ability to take risks. To this end, Barratt reviewed and analyzed the instrument in his factorial studies (Alvarez, 2011).

Pechorro, Oliveira, Gonçalves and Jesus (2017), postulate that the scale is a valid and reliable self-reporting instrument for impulsiveness assessment. The scale is composed of 18 questions quoted on an ordinal scale that vary from Rarely/Never to Almost always/Semprety, so that the higher scores indicate a greater presence of impulsivity.

According to Garcia (2018), the Barratt Impulsiveness Scale was developed in 1959 and has been considered the most recognized self-reported measure of impulsiveness in both research and clinical practice. At first, the author proposed that impulsivity and anxiety would represent characteristics of the orthogonal personality. BIS-11 in its original form has been validated by Patton, Stanford and Barratt (1995) and its original version has been translated into at least eleven other languages.

Currently, the scale is in its eleventh revision. Barratt (1959) when conceiving the current model for impulsivity evaluation presented 30 items of self-reporting so that they could opportune the analysis of the individual behavior of the subject classifying it as: 1=rarely or never; 2= from time to time; 3=frequently; 4 = almost always/without. The scale scores range from 30 to 120 points, so that the higher values reveal the presence of impulsive behaviors.

Pereira (2014) describes the items belonging to Barratt's Impulsivity Scale according to the types of impulsivity. According to the author, the statements concerning the behavior that comprise the items: 2, 3, 4, 16, 17, 19, 21, 22, 23, 25 and 30 are related to motor impulsivity. The items 6, 5, 9, 11, 20, 26, 28 are related to the type of attentional impulsivity. For the type of impulsivity that refers to non-planning the items are: 1, 7,10, 12, 13, 14, 15, 18, 27, 19. The author highlights that items 1, 7, 8, 9, 10, 12, 13, 15, 20, 29 and 30 must be inverted for the calculation of partial and total values.

Also according to the author, BIS-11 means the latest efforts by Barratt and other authors to measure an impulsivity construct that is orthogonal to anxiety, associated with personality characteristics such as extrovert behavior and search for sensation. BIS-11 is composed of three sub-scales: attentional impulsiveness, motor impulsiveness, and lack of planning. These subscales are related to the following components: motor: related to the lack of inhibition of incoherent responses; attentional that is associated with rapid decision making; and the lack of planning that refers to behaviors that are oriented towards the present. This model has proved to be reliable and with valid criteria when used in surveys that seek to analyze Impulsivity.

The statements to be answered are determined on Barratt's Impulsivity Scale - Bis 11, so that actions vary from never to always. However, by stating that the action always happens or almost always, the existence of a consecutive practice that represents a maximum tendency to impulsivity has been asserted (Barratt, 1959).

Analyzing the studies of Brito-Costa, Moisão; Briegas and Castro (2019), the BIS-11, Barratt's Impulsivity Scale - is a Likert type self-response scale with four points and in them are distributed 30 statements that determine the manifestations of impulsivity. The scale has a quotation of 30 to 120 points, so that the higher the quotation, the higher the incidence of impulsive behavior. Its results are global and the calculations allowed are partial and refer to 1st and 2nd order factors. In addition, there are also reverse quotation items. The author also states that the scale has a good alpha reliability of Cronbach of 0.82 in its original version.

In other words, the *Barratt impulsiveness scale-youth (BIS-youth)* or Barratt Impulsivity *Scale*, is a tool in the form of a questionnaire that aims to evaluate impulsivity. It contains 30 questions of the Likert scale type and presents a choice of several answers: "(1) never/rarely; (2) sometimes; (3) frequently; (4) almost always/always" (Patton, Stanford& Barratt, 1995; Otto, 2016).

Malloy-Diniz et al (2010) states that Barratt's Impulsivity scale score ranges from 30 to 120 points, with high scores indicating the presence of impulsive behavior. It also presents an overall score, the BIS-11 which is intended to calculate the partial scores related to three subdomains of impulsivity.

Brito-Costa, Moisão; Briegas and Castro (2019, p. 2), argue that many researchers are concerned with the search for scientific evidence on the components that integrate impulsivity-related phenomena, in addition to being concerned with their measurement. However, this is a complex issue that has generated not only consensual opinions of authors and researchers but also a subject of much controversy. In view of this, a lot of research and empirical validation is required.

Starting from a multidimensional conception of impulsiveness, Barratt argued about the existence of three distinct components: (1) Motor: related to non-inhibition of incoherent responses; (2) Ascension: related to rapid decision making and; (3) Lack of planning: present oriented behaviors (Patton, Stanford & Barrat, 1995).

According to Brito-Costa, Moisão; Briegas and Castro (2019), the factors are grouped into types of behavior: Self-control behavior, planning, attention and perseverance. Their psychometric indicators are reliable and can be applied both in empirical studies and to assist in evaluations and interventions in the field of psychology, specifically of a cognitive-behavioral nature. As regards the analysis of psychometric properties, EIB-11 can be considered an empirically feasible tool to assist in measuring the impulsiveness of individuals, taking into account the factors outlined above.

The attentional component defined by Barratt (1959) is related to rapid decision making, which characterizes impulsiveness. Thus, individuals who in the purchasing decision making process act thoughtlessly, without considering what might happen in the future, or if they really have conditions to fulfill such financial commitment are within the emphatic scope of the attentional component. The act of doing things in an immediate way, without having time to reflect, as well as the purchase without planning or in an inconsequent way, ends up leading the individual to decide for the acquisition of a certain object or service without having been planned. Such an attitude is related to the component of the proposed model that tends to impulsiveness and consequently to indebtedness.

This Barratt scale is of the Likert type and the presented score favours the values to be calculated, according to the model proposed by Barratt (1959). For this author, the proposed measure is adequate to evaluate the impulsive subject's propensity to indebtedness since the non-planning refers to an unforeseen behavior, peculiar to impulsiveness of purchase. This behavior is centered on one of the 03 distinct components that refers to lack of planning: behaviors oriented to the present.

In this sense, impulsivity is understood as an intricate phenotype characterized by different cognitive and behavioral patterns, directing the organism towards immediate and medium/long term dysfunctional consequences (cf. Malloy-Diniz et al, 2010).

Thus, there are various losses resulting from the different manifestations of impulsiveness that can occur in various day-to-day situations. Whether due to mental disorders or not, there is a need to invest in the search for evaluation, preventive measures and treatment.

Brito-Costa, Moisão, Briegas and Castro (2019, p. 6) consider that "the EIB-11 is an appropriate tool for its reliability (α =0.762) and validity with which investigations can be carried out in different fields". However, it is important that caution is taken when used both in clinical practice and in forensic research and practice.

In addition, evaluators cannot create hasty conclusions based solely on price indexes, and should therefore make a full evaluation, considering other individual characteristics, also counting on other variables. It should be noted that the Barratt scale only presents clues in relation to the phenomenon of impulsiveness of the subjects.

Given the importance and relevance of the model proposed by Barratt (1959), impulsivity/personality oriented researches, from the end of the 50's, seek to contribute their arguments to the author's theoretical basis, since he was the pioneer in the creation and development of the evaluation instrument used to distinguish the different traits of impulsivity.

Patton, Stanford and Barrat (1995) also contribute in the creation of Barratt's (1959) scale to argue that motor impulsivity is an indication of whether or not the subject has the capacity to inhibit his behavior and whether he acts according to the circumstances of the moment, because as Barratt (1959) pointed out, cognitive impulsivity has a connection with the individual's ability to concentrate, that is, whether he is capable of performing a certain task.

For the above-mentioned authors, impulsiveness is considered unplanned when the individual does not reflect before performing his actions, i.e., acts without planning. Analyzing from this point of view, it is understood that indebtedness is related to this type of behavior and inserted in one of the components of the model proposed by Barratt (1959).

With this, the most used and most reliable self-reporting instrument nowadays, which serves to evaluate impulsiveness according to what is found in the literature and based on experiments, is the Barratt Impulsiveness Scale - 11 (BIS-11). Barratt (1959), when he idealized his initial version aimed to evaluate impulsivity considering it as a personality trait.

New researches appeared and these, therefore, could identify a structure in multidimension characterized by 06 factors that received the name of "first order" understood by: attention, cognitive instability, motor and perseverance, self-control and cognitive complexity. These in turn came in 03 factors of second order, called: attention, motor and non-planning (Barratt, 1965).

In this sense, Neves (2013) states that according to Barratt's model impulsivity refers to a construction of personality, orthogonal to the dimension of personality and anxiety, and can be divided into three components.

3 OBJECTIVES

3.1 GENERAL OBJECTIVE

To verify the correlation between impulsiveness and attitude to indebtedness in subjects of the adult population of the municipality of Natal - RN.

3.2 SPECIFIC OBJECTIVES

(1) Check the psychometric quality of the measures used: the impulsivity scale in the adult population of Natal - RN;

(2) Assess the psychometic quality of the debt attitude scale

(3) Correlate impulsivity and attitude to indebtedness;

Based on these objectives, the following assumptions are made:

H1: the impulsivity variable is expected to be directly related to the attitude of indebtedness;

H2: those research participants with the highest impulsivity score are expected to have a higher debt score.

4 METHODS

4.1 SAMPLE

It will be a quantitative, descriptive, exploratory and correlational survey, in which people from the general population in the city of Natal-RN participated.

The reference sample was evaluated in the G Power 3.1 statistical package, which is used to calculate the statistical power by relating the '*n*' required for the research and type of calculation to be performed (Faul, Erdfelder, Lang, & Buchner, 2007).

Data collection was carried out in a non-probabilistic way, using the snowball method, because the availability and interest of the respondent in participating in the survey was considered. For this, a probability of 95% ($p < 0.05$), magnitude of the sample effect (r $0.\geq 50$) and a hypothetical power pattern (π $0.\geq 80$) designed to verify the quality and significance of the sample for conducting the survey were considered.

To meet the main objective of this study, based on the criteria established in Gpower, a sample of 112 subjects revealed to be sufficient for the survey, which presented the following statistical indicators in relation to sample quality: t $1\geq.98$, π $0\geq.93$, $p < 0.05$. Such sample is not only sufficient for the study in question, but also reveals a condition for performing statistical calculations related to the objective of the survey.

Regarding the inclusion criteria for survey participants, the following are highlighted: age over 18, people willing to collaborate with the survey by answering the questionnaire sent through digital platform, be economically active, belong to any social class, and receive monthly over one minimum wage.

The cut-off regarding the minimum wage was due to the understanding that to be an active consumer it is necessary for the individual to have some financial source and as income threshold, the "minimum wage" was taken as a reference due to the requirement imposed by the retail trade that in order to obtain credit or term purchases it is necessary to prove income. This requirement also determines the possibility of analyzing the impulsiveness and indebtedness criteria in these individuals, since they have the purchasing power.

Furthermore, it is also recognized that from the legal point of view, the minimum wage is the minimum amount that the employer must pay the employee, in the exercise of an employment contract, for his performance in normal working hours, and that, according to market prices, this financial importance may be sufficient for the subsistence of the employee.

4.2 RESEARCH TOOLS

4.2.1 BARRATT IMPULSIVITY SCALE - BIS -11.

It is a valid and reliable self-reporting scale for impulsivity evaluation. It consists of 30 questions of the Likert scale type and presents a choice of several answers: "(1) never/rarely; (2) sometimes; (3) frequently; (4) almost always/ever" (Patton, Stanford, & Barratt, 1995; Otto, 2016).

Starting from a multidimensional conception of impulsiveness, it is argued that there are three distinct components capable of measuring this construct: (1) Motor, related to non-inhibition of incoherent responses; (2) Attentiveness or Attention, which refers to rapid decision making and; (3) Lack of planning: behaviors oriented to the present (Patton, Stanford & Barratt, 1995).

Malloy-Diniz et al (2010) states that Barratt's Impulsivity scale score ranges from 30 to 120 points, with high scores indicating the presence of impulsive behavior. It also presents an overall score, the BIS-11 which is intended to calculate the partial scores related to three subdomains of impulsivity.

4.2.2 DICKMAN IMPULSIVITY SCALE

This is an inventory, originally developed in English, by J. Dickman in the 90s, last century. It was translated and adapted to Brazilian Portuguese by Gomes (2016) and consists of 23 items, distributed in two dimensions: functional and dysfunctional impulsiveness.

In this book, the same instrument adapted for the Brazilian context was used, but in its reduced version of the original proposal, that is, a scale with 18 items. The respondent should indicate his or her response related to the items (for example: 1. I don't spend much time thinking about a situation before acting; 2. I try to avoid activities in which I have to act without much time to think before; 3. I don't like to make decisions quickly, even simple decisions like choosing what to wear or what to eat for dinner; 4. I like to solve problems slowly and carefully, etc.), on a Likert scale of five points (see Annex III).

4.2.3 INDEBTEDNESS SCALE

The Attitude Scale to Indebtedness was developed by the authors of the book, which was inspired by the proposal of Lea, Webley and Walker (1995). Due to the lack of clarity and of an approach to the evaluation of psychological construction, it was decided to create a measure that would be able to evaluate issues related to indebtedness, but that would emphasize the attitudes of staff towards consumption regarding the use of money, planning, term consumption, loans with friends, among others, as well as to associate with financial life and the possibility of carrying out activities predisposed to consumption.

With this, the scale was composed of nine items (for example: 1- For you, it is normal for people to be in debt to pay their bills; 2 - You prefer to pay in installments even if in total it is more expensive; 3 - You prefer to buy in installments than expect to have money to buy in cash; 4- It is okay to have debt if you know you can pay, etc.).

To measure this type of construction, a likert scale of five points was used (1 = I totally disagree; 2 = I disagree; 3 = indifferent; 4 = I agree; 5 = I totally agree), where the higher the point marked, the greater will also be the attitude to indebtedness.

In addition to these scales, participants answered a demographic and socioeconomic questionnaire composed of questions related to age, gender, marital status, number of dependents in the family, housing condition and economic income. Also, questions related to the behaviour of indebtedness were included, for example: consumption that compromises economic income, for which the respondent should indicate, on a five-point scale ranging from 0 = no compromise to 4 = total compromise; income compromise due to similar purchases, in this variable the personnel should indicate if little or a lot, on a five-point scale from 0 to 4 as well.

4.3 ETHICAL PROCEDURES AND DATA ANALYSIS

All the procedures adopted in this research followed the guidelines set forth in Resolution 466/2012 of the CNS and in Resolution 016/2000 of the Federal Council of Psychology for research with human beings (National Health Council [CNS], 2012; National Association for Research and Post-Graduation in Psychology [ANPEPP], 2000), submitted to CONEP and approved by CAAE research protocol No. 21344719.3.0000.5537.

After the collection and having the data grouped and saved in spreadsheet in the statistics program SPSS for Windows (version 24.0), were analyzed in addition to the test of normality sample, a descriptive statistics and analysis of Cronbach's Alpha, Pearson's correlations, Student's t test, exploratory factor analysis of the main components and Anova

Regarding the exploratory factor analysis, some items were considered with the purpose of confirming, adjusting the relevant factors and assisting in the interpretation of the data, following the theories proposed by Malhotras (2011), Hair, Anderson, Tatham and Black (2008). These are them: Apha de Conbrach, communality, KMO, Varimax rotation, Bartlett sphericity test, mean and standard deviation.

Thus, the KMO (one of the main items cited) was intended to measure the adequacy of factor analysis, in which values between 0.5 and 1.0 considers the appropriate analysis. Values below 0.50 signal inadequate factorial analysis. The KMO evaluates the phenomenon provoked by a certain correlation between pairs of variables which are influenced by other variables. In small values it means that they cannot be explained by another, already above 0.70 means the desirable (Hair, Anderson, Tatham, & Black, 2008).

Later, the Bartlett sphericity test was used to measure and evaluate the hypothesis that variables can correlate with the population. Being the result value $r = 1$, it means that the variable relates to itself, independently; at $r = 0$, it presents an interrelationship with the others.

It should also be noted that the factor analysis procedure includes the Varimax rotation analysis, which is a method capable of minimizing the number of variables with a high degree of a factor, thus expanding the knowledge that contributes to improvements in factor interpretation. Hair et al (2009) states that the Varimax method is considerably relevant in comparison to other methods, since it presents efficient criteria to achieve a simplified factorial structure.

In short, the factorial analysis starts from the need for a study arising from the research problem. Its main objective is to summarize or condense the information involved in several variables in order to facilitate understanding and define the important constructs to explain the phenomenon beyond the dimensions assumed and characteristics of the original variables (Hair et al., 2009).

5 RESULTS

Finished the data collection time, the answers were categorized, in the Excell program, from nominal to interval. Carried through this stage, it was opted to verify, from an exploration analysis, the data that were part of the sample, which, typed in the spreadsheet of the SPSS; in this phase of the research, it was carried through through a visual inspection in the maximum and minimum values of the scales and soon after it was verified the condition of the minimum criteria that attended to the assumptions of the calculations of representativity and reliability of the used measures.

Regarding the information on the sample, it presented the following characteristics: 112 subjects from the municipality of Natal - RN, with all employees, distributed in public and private organizations, having a higher frequency (66%) of the respondents belonging to both sectors, men (41%) and women (59%), aged 24 to 77 years (M = 43.69, d.p. = 11.18), 64% were married, all of them indicated having above a minimum wage.

Regarding the dynamics of family organization, 54% do not have dependents living with them, 67% have their own house. In relation to bank credit, 52% has a home, car, etc. financing, and 32% has college and professional project financing.

Regarding the behavior of indebtedness, only 24% have chronic debts, the others (86%) have small debts and/or some of them at the end of the discharge. As for the behavior of buying in installments 26% states that they buy a lot, 20% moderately, but 54% indicated not to adhere. For 29% of respondents, their buying habits compromised their income, 22% moderately and 49% had no commitment. Finally, as for repentant behavior when buying for no reason, 57% said they were not repentant, but 32% felt very sorry.

5.1 NORMALITY CHECK OF THE SAMPLE

Before meeting the objectives established in the book, statistical analyses were performed regarding the quality of the sample; thus, in relation to the data missing from the surveys, it was observed that they were below the percentage of 5%. Considering this information, it is possible to replace them by the mean or mode of the sample data, if there is some empty space or double typing in the grid of data insertion in the statistical program (cf. Tabachnick & Fidell, 2001).

Regarding the multicollinearity among the variables, the correlations among them were within the parameters defined by Tabachnick and Fidell (2001) [r ≤ 0.90, ranging from 0.32 to 0.69], revealing that there are no variables with a high degree of correlation, which allows the generation of models with low measurement error. The presence of multivariate outliers was verified in the sample; this was performed through the Kolmogorov-Smirnov (KS) normality test, intended for analysis of samples larger than 100 subjects, a normality (KS = 0.52) of the sample at a $p < 0.24$ was observed.

We also evaluated the differences in asymmetry through histograms with superimposition of the normal curve and asymmetry indices. Based on the orientation of the statistical parameters defined by Miles and Shevlin (2001), who established that even finding in the sample data a possible normal distribution, observing a statistical indicator of asymmetry smaller than 1.0, it is still possible to consider it acceptable. Thus, when evaluating the asymmetry indices of the measurements, all the asymmetry values found remained within the acceptable parameters, which ranged from -1.19 to 1.56.

However, it is necessary to point out in this book that both independent (VI) and dependent (VD) variables measure the opinions of the same respondents in the survey, a condition that suggests finding a *common* method *variance* (VCM), which can become a serious problem because, if statistically represented, respondents probably did not respond based on the evaluation suggested in the items of each construct.

For this, a Harman factor test was used to examine the existence of some common method bias (variance) in the collected data, as suggested by Podsakoff, MacKenzie and Podsakoff (2003). It was observed, therefore, the existence of a single factor with autovalue above 1.00, explaining less than 50% of the sample, that is, 32.58% of the covariance between the variables, implying the inexistence of the common variance problem of the method.

We also tested the non-response tendency, through which the differences between the first (n1 = 10) and the last (n2 = 10) participants of the survey were evaluated; through the Levene test, which is intended to verify the equality of variances and a t test to evaluate the equality of the means of the scores between the groups (n1 and n2) it was observed that there were no significant results at a level of 5% between the mean scores of the constructions (with $t \leq 1.96$).

From this result, it is possible to highlight that there is no non-response bias, which represents not a significant problem of the measure in the subjects collected and in the responses of the constructs. Once the quality of the measures and of the constructs in question was confirmed, we tried to proceed to evaluate the specific objectives of the book, which were presented in the next sections.

The assessment with this condition was motivated by the following reasons: (1) It is suggested that this is a pioneer research with the adult population of the municipality of Natal - RN, with a specific approach on this subject; (2) - There is no Brazilian scientific publication in the area of organizational and work psychology, health in general, among others. during the period of July 2018 to January 2019, on platforms such as: scielo.br, newpsi.bvs-psi.org.br, pepsic.bvsalud.org, with content and focus related to the theme; (3) - There is a need to verify these measures, since more than two years have passed since their use in research on the theme, a condition that requires a verification of the consistency of such measure, based on the social and political context of the research.

5.2 DISCRIMINATION AND REPRESENTATIVENESS OF THE CONTENT OF THE SCALES ITEMS USED IN THEBOOK

In order to identify the relationship between theoretical and empirical perspective of the content of the items in the scales used, we took as orientation the psychometric proposals of the items highlighted, respectively, by Pechorro, Oliveira, Gonçalves and Jesus (2017) for the impulsivity scale of Barratt and Gomes (2016) for the impulsivity scale of Dickman; regarding the scale of indebtedness attitude, this also went through such statistical analysis, with the purpose of filtering the distribution of the items in factors, since it is an original instrument and still, not intended for psychological evaluation, but only for opinion polls and/or economic 'behavior' (cf. SPC, 2015, Pacheco, Campara & Costa, 2017; PEIC, 2017).

In this way, both the discrimination of the items were initially verified, evaluating the relationship between their terms and their previously established behavior-domain representativeness, as well as the representativeness of content. These steps are based on evaluation, systematically verify the theoretical relationship of the test and the situations specified in the items and how much they represent the expected aspects (cf. Formiga, Fleury, Fandiño & Souza, 2016).

Thus, in Table 1, of the indebtedness attitude scale, as a better organization for reading the results, the discriminatory power and the representativeness of the content of the items of the said scale were evaluated; in this section of calculations, the main objective is to evaluate a greater specificity in the statistical analysis for the organization and verification of the distribution of the items of the scale in question.

Theoretical analysis is based on the assumptions of the Classical Theory of Testing (TCT) (cf. Formiga, & Souza, 2016). That is, according to Pasquali (2011), the need for this calculation is due to the following question: are the items able to discriminate the answers of people with close magnitudes? That is, do they discriminate those of the lower and upper groups in relation to the measured construct?

To meet this hypothetical-methodological condition (the discrimination and representativeness of the items on the scales), a total score of the said scale was calculated and then its median; respondents with scores below the median were classified as the lower group, while those with scores above the median were defined as the upper group (cf. Formiga, Fleury, Fandiño & Souza, 2016).

Considering each of the items in the measurement, a t test was performed for independent samples and both groups were compared, observing which of the items in the scale discriminate people with statistically close magnitudes (Table 1).

Table 1 : Discrimination (t) and representativity of content (r) of the indebtedness scale items.

Items	Groups	Media	d.p.	t	p-value <	r
Attitude Indebtedness1	gi	1,49	0,836	-3,35	0,01	0,51*
	gs	2,22	1,346			
Attitude Indebtedness2	gi	1,98	1,194	-5,21	0,01	0,57*
	gs	3,31	1,435			
Attitude Indebtedness3	gi	1,40	0,683	-4,32	0,01	0,50*
	gs	2,31	1,393			
Attitude Indebtedness4	gi	1,89	1,117	-6,75	0,01	0,54*
	gs	3,51	1,347			
Attitude Indebtedness5	gi	4,63	0,958	-1,91	0,10	0,24*
	gs	4,88	0,588			
Attitude Indebtedness6	gi	2,65	1,250	-1,18	0,23	0,19
	gs	2,96	1,414			
Attitude Indebtedness7	gi	4,15	1,053	0,41	0,67	0,07
	gs	4,06	1,139			
Attitude Indebtedness8	gi	4,22	1,150	-2,18	0,01	0,57*
	gs	4,63	0,720			
Attitude Indebtedness9	gi	4,69	0,791	-1,23	0,22	0,17
	gs	4,86	0,633			

Note: * $p < 0.05$; r = Pearson correlation; t = Student test

In table 6, it is possible to highlight that, of the nine items, only five (namely: 1, 2, 3, 4 and 8), not only presented a $t \geq 1.96$, but were also significant. Thus, capable of discriminating the scores that the respondents in each of the items of the construct approached were positioned in the scale; it can be stated that in these items, the respondents understood what the content established by the author who developed the measure established theoretically.

Also in table 6, we see the representativity of the items-factor content, indicated by Pearson's 'r'. From the calculation of Pearson's correlation (r), which aims to evaluate the relationship of the items of the scale with the total score of the same, condition which is expected to be significant and have correlations above 0.50 (cf. Ant, Fleury, Fandiño & Souza, 2016). The reason for considering this minimum threshold for correlational assessment in the representativeness of content, is due to such score, being in the range of interpretation. This condition suggests the possibility that it is possible to affirm the empirical approximation between the variables, which, theoretically mortgaged.

Thus established, from Pearson's correlation calculation (r), in the same table, it is possible to observe the existence of an item-building relationship, which, of the nine items, only five were significant and positive, being above 0.50. It can be highlighted that, of all these items, five of them represent the proposal of the construction of a scale that evaluates the attitude of indebtedness.

Regarding the other scales, Barratt's impulsivity scale underwent similar statistical analysis. Considering the same statistical limit (i.e., t > 1.96 and r > 0.50), both Student's t test and Pearson's correlation were performed, respectively, to assess item discrimination and content representativity. In table 2, below, it is possible to observe that out of the total of 30 items, only for 16 of them it is possible to state that they discriminate and represent the impulsivity construct; such condition suggests the retention of these when it is intended to organize the sum of the construct in its total score and distribution of factors.

Table 2 : Discrimination (t) and content representativity (r) of the items on the Barratt Impulsivity scale.

Items	groups	Average	d.p.	t	p-value <	r
IMPULBARR1	gi	2,69	0,690	-1,54	0,12	0,12
	gs	2,92	0,860			
IMPULBARR2	gi	1,60	0,564	-3,59	0,001	0,54*
	gs	2,02	0,641			
IMPULBARR3	gi	2,15	0,731	-2,91	0,001	0,55*
	gs	2,60	0,869			
IMPULBARR4	gi	1,53	0,742	-0,98	0,32	0,16
	gs	1,67	0,785			
IMPULBARR5	gi	1,71	0,712	-2,34	0,001	0,53*
	gs	2,06	0,826			
IMPULBARR6	gi	1,62	0,623	-7,04	0,001	0,65*
	gs	2,71	0,957			
IMPULBARR7	gi	2,25	0,985	-2,87	0,001	0,53*
	gs	2,83	1,080			
IMPULBARR8	gi	2,93	0,723	0,02	0,98	0,03
	gs	2,92	0,763			
IMPULBARR9	gi	2,49	0,814	0,63	0,52	0,03
	gs	2,38	0,911			
IMPULBARR10	gi	2,15	0,951	-1,03	0,45	0,17
	gs	2,54	1,056			
IMPULBARR11	gi	1,35	0,615	-2,36	0,001	0,50*
	gs	1,73	1,031			
IMPULBARR12	gi	2,96	0,637	0,02	0,98	0,06
	gs	2,96	0,740			
IMPULBARR13	gi	2,85	0,920	-1,25	0,21	0,18
	gs	3,08	0,926			
IMPULBARR14	gi	1,67	0,546	-3,23	0,001	0,53*
	gs	2,08	0,737			
IMPULBARR15	gi	1,56	0,739	-4,59	0,001	0,59*
	gs	2,37	1,048			
IMPULBARR16	gi	1,25	0,480	-0,64	0,52	0,20
	gs	1,33	0,678			
IMPULBARR17	gi	1,64	0,649	-3,39	0,001	0,51*
	gs	2,12	0,808			
IMPULBARR18	gi	1,69	0,742	-2,77	0,001	0,52*
	gs	2,13	0,908			
IMPULBARR19	gi	1,58	0,599	-4,56	0,001	0,54*
	gs	2,15	0,697			
IMPULBARR20	gi	2,60	0,627	-0,52	0,59	0,16
	gs	2,67	0,785			
IMPULBARR21	gi	1,20	0,404	-0,31	0,89	0,21
	gs	1,21	0,498			
IMPULBARR22	gi	1,73	0,757	-1,42	0,05	0,28
	gs	2,10	0,823			
IMPULBARR23	gi	1,85	0,756	-0,77	0,47	0,15
	gs	1,98	1,038			
IMPULBARR24	gi	1,53	0,663	-3,19	0,001	0,52*

	gs	2,00	0,863			
IMPULBARR25	gi	1,49	0,663	-0,33	0,76	0,05
	gs	1,54	0,959			
IMPULBARR26	gi	2,47	0,879	-3,97	0,001	0,56*
	gs	3,13	0,841			
IMPULBARR27	gi	2,00	0,745	-1,74	0,08	0,16
	gs	2,29	0,936			
IMPULBARR28	gi	1,65	0,645	-3,40	0,001	0,57*
	gs	2,21	1,016			
IMPULBARR29	gi	2,33	0,924	-2,01	0,001	0,52*
	gs	2,52	1,038			
IMPULBARR30	gi	2,78	0,896	-2,47	0,001	0,52*
	gs	2,87	0,908			

Note: * p-value < 0.05; r = Pearson correlation; t = Student test.

Regarding the Dickman impulsivity scale, after performing the Student t-test to verify item discrimination and Pearson's correlation to assess content representativeness, it was observed that of the 18 items proposed, only 11 of these were significant both to discriminate and represent the content of the items presented to respondents.

Thus, only items 2, 3, 6, 7, 8, 9, 10, 12, 13, 16 and 18, were filtered in both calculations (in the discrimination, this had the t above 1.92 and in the representativity, presented scores above 0.50), which suggest from the results, keep such items in the analysis of the construct. As shown in

Table 3 : Discrimination (t) and content representativity (r) of Dickman Impulsivity scale items.

Items	groups	Average	d.p.	t	p-value <	r
Impulsivity	gi	2,44	1,128	-1,92	0,06	0,11
Dickman1	gs	2,87	1,150			
Impulsivity	gi	2,94	, 867	-3,06	0,01	0,50*
Dickman2	gs	3,56	1,160			
Impulsivity	gi	2,35	1,214	-5,24	0,01	0,57*
Dickman3	gs	3,63	1,278			
Impulsivity	gi	3,29	1,154	-1,58	0,12	0,19
Dickman4	gs	3,65	1,135			
Impulsivity	gi	2,06	1,190	-0,22	0,82	0,04
Dickman5	gs	2,11	1,223			
Impulsivity	gi	2,41	1,252	-2,58	0,01	0,57*
Dickman6	gs	2,81	1,333			
Impulsivity	gi	2,69	1,288	-3,52	0,01	0,53*
Dickman7	gs	3,56	1,369			
Impulsivity	gi	2,55	1,137	-2,52	0,01	0,50*
Dickman8	gs	3,17	1,356			
Impulsivity	gi	1,68	1,058	-3,16	0,01	0,50*
Dickman9	gs	2,41	1,267			
Impulsivity	gi	3,44	1,198	-2,25	0,01	0,56*
Dickman10	gs	3,72	1,089			
Impulsivity	gi	2,42	1,197	-1,72	0,08	0,15
Dickman11	gs	2,87	1,428			
Impulsivity	gi	1,96	0,856	-4,57	0,01	0,57*
Dickman12	gs	2,94	1,309			
Impulsivity	gi	1,74	0,899	-4,48	0,01	0,53*
Dickman13	gs	2,67	1,197			
Impulsivity	gi	3,28	1,031	-0,85	0,39	0,14
Dickman14	gs	3,46	1,161			
Impulsivity	gi	2,92	1,047	-1,14	0,26	0,11
Dickman15	gs	3,17	1,209			
Impulsivity	gi	2,18	1,034	-2,92	0,01	0,51*
Dickman16	gs	2,61	1,220			
Impulsivity	gi	3,82	1,024	-0,74	0,46	0,16
Dickman17	gs	3,96	0,951			
Impulsivity	gi	3,52	1,129	-2,41	0,01	0,57*
Dickman18	gs	3,83	1,129			

Note: * p-value < 0.05; r = Pearson correlation; t = Student test

From these results it can be stated that the respondents recognize the items of each of the constructs, but not in their general set, which was proposed by the above-mentioned authors.

It is necessary to consider that only those significant items can be maintained when one intends to analyze the constructs evaluated in this book, because they point in the direction of semantic agreement items-constructs, since in the scales, the subjects scored in the form expected, when related to the discrimination of items (t ≥ 1.96) and in the representativity of content (r ≥ 0.50), thus offering greater security to the constructs approached, thus suggesting to use in the evaluation of this phenomenon through these scales, only the items highlighted.

But, a reflection could be highlighted: having the results presenting a reduction in the quantity of items in each construction, when compared to the original measure, would it not be necessary to perform a factor analysis? In thesis, it is not necessary, therefore, to take as a reference of the evaluation for the already existing constructs, both the axiomatic proposal of the psychological evaluation of the referred phenomena, as well as, the theoretical direction expressed by the authors who defend the definition and measurement of the psychological evaluation of impulsiveness.

Recognized through these calculations, that the research subjects were able to cognitively represent the content and meaning of the items related to the constructs discussed in this book, the next step was to verify the internal consistency of the scales, a result that will be presented below.

For considering that only two scales have their theoretical and factorial organization very clear, for example, Pechorro, Oliveira, Gonçalves and Jesus (2017), which, presented three factors for Barratt's impulsivity scale, while in Gomes' study (2016) only two factors for Dickman's impulsivity scale). Regarding the debt attitude scale, an exploratory factorial analysis will be conducted for this one.

5.3 INTERNAL CONSISTENCY (ALPHA) AND INTRACLASS CORRELATION (ICC) OF THE TWO IMPULSIVITY SCALES

Regarding the reliability of the scales, according to Hair, Anderson, Tatham and Black (2008), it is necessary to evaluate through a psychometric indicator whether the measurement used is consistent with the measurement of the concept of the construct to be measured.

Even finding, in studies previous to the one developed in the book, the use of this psychometric indicator brings more benefits than scientific tautology, because, the more one knows the alphas indicators in temporal, contextual and sample terms of a measure, the more one is guaranteeing the theoretical and empirical quality of the researcher who developed the instrument; thus, it is known that it has traditionally used the Cronbach alpha (α) (it should be $0 \geq .70$, but also values up to 0.60 are acceptable) to verify the consistency of an instrument in the administered sample context.

In the statistical package SPSSWIN, the Cronbach alpha was calculated; in table 4, it can be seen that the alphas were above 0.70 for both scales used in the book. The findings in this study revealed results that guaranteed the reliability of impulsivity measurements. Thus, the alphas for each construct evaluated were above the expected psychometric criteria guaranteeing the consistency of the constructs in the sample collected (Hair, Anderson, Tatham & Black, 2008; Hutz, Bandeira, & Trentini, 2015).

From the results of the alphas, it is possible to affirm that the scales administered in this book measure in a homogeneous way the relation concept-to-measure proposed by the authors of the mentioned measures, however, considering a reduced version. Attention is drawn to the maintenance of the variation of alphas (V), which remained close to the previous observation, confirming the homogeneity of this indicator even when the need to exclude items that could interfere in the quality of the measurements was indicated in the calculation.

Thus, for both measures, it suggests to consider when the impulsivity in a sample with the characteristics observed in this book is to be evaluated, to administer the reduced version (see table 5).

Table 4 : Cronbach alphas scores (α) of the scales administered to adults in the municipality of Natal - RN

Buildings	Alfa de Cronbach			ICC (IC 95%)	p-value <
	αgeneral	Vα	F Friedman		
Impulsivity Barratt (original version)	0,64	0,61-0,72	61,39	0,67 (0,67-0,71)	0,01
Impulsivity Barratt (book version	0,75	0,70-0,77	78,83	0,75 (0,71-0,79)	0,001
Impulsivity Dickman (original version)	0,68	0,67-0,73	2,27	0,69 (0,69-0,73)	0,01
Impulsivity Dickman (book version)	0,74	0,69-0,76	2,84	0,74 (0,71-0,75)	0,001

Notes: Vα = Alpha Variation when item is excluded; F = Friedman Test; ICC = Intraclass Correlation.

Thus, based on these calculations, it can be stated that the scales used in this book, besides representing well the content proposed by the aforementioned authors regarding impulsiveness, were reliable; it should be noted that not only in the discrimination of the items, as well as in the evaluation of their representativity, in which there were, respectively, significant differences and high correlations (above 0.50) and also, with indicators of reliability of these measures revealing safety for the theoretical-empirical set addressed in this book.

In general, the psychometric conditions established in this stage of analysis of the results, allow confidence in the measures and the evaluation of the problem phenomenon related to impulsiveness.

Answered to the specific objectives and hypotheses, such steps were necessary due to the lack of studies that evaluated these instruments with the specificity of the sample collected for this book.

It then tried to respond to an additional objective, for which they had as a central hypothesis the unifatorialization of the scale of indebtedness attitude, previously pointed out in the analysis of the discrimination and representativeness of the items, this result will be presented in the next section.

5.4 EXPLORATORY FACTORIAL ANALYSIS OF THE ATTITUDE SCALE OF DEBT

Based on the results of the discrimination and content representativeness of the debt attitude scale (EAE), an exploratory factor analysis was carried out in order to verify the factoriality of this measure in question.

For this, a factorial analysis was performed, in which the calculation was performed using the Main Components Factorial Method (PC), leaving free the number of factors to be extracted, without rotation and assuming saturation of ± 0.30.

In order to make a more secure decision in the choice of factors, the following criteria have been adopted: (1) amount of own values (eigenvalues) equal or superior to 1 (Kaiser Criterion), (2) graphical distribution of own values, taking as reference the point from which no other factor contributes considerably to the structure (Cattell Criterion) and (3) parallel analysis (O'Connor, 2000; Dancey & Reidy, 2006).

Once the factor evaluation criteria were defined, the results of the analyses identified the adequacy of the correlation matrix: KMO = 0.78 and the Bartlett Sphericity Test, $\chi 2/gl= 93.28/15$, $p< 0.001$. In the graphical distribution based on own values (Cattell's criterion), two factors were identified in the scale (see Figure 3).

Figure 3 : Slope diagram of the number of factors plotted from the EAE.

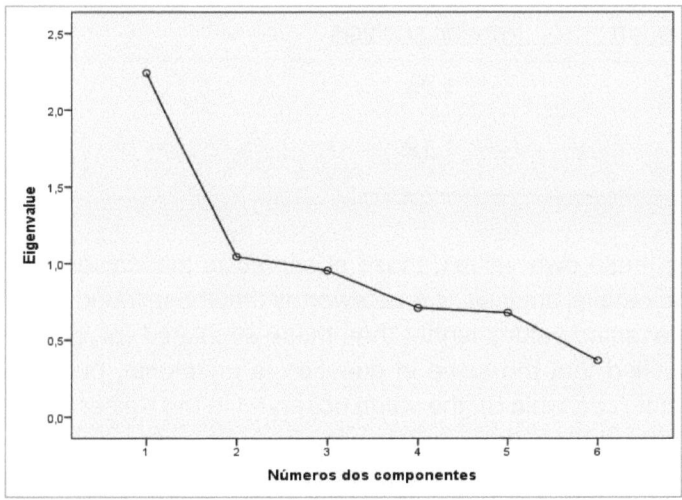

According to Kaiser's criterion (that is, the own values - Eigenvalues), it was also identified the existence of two factors with own values greater than 1 (one), explaining together 54.75% of the total variance of the measured phenomenon.

In order to have no doubts about the factorial organization of the EAE, the parallel analysis was performed, assuming the same parameters of the original database. That is, 112 participants and six (ten) variables, having their own values generated in 1,000 random simulations with the items (See Table 6).

Table 5 : Distribution of PC analysis factors according to Kaiser's criteria and parallel analysis

Kaiser Criterion	Parallel analysis
2,24	1,24
1,05	1,12

Comparing these own values, those observed in the Kaiser criteria and those of the parallel analysis, it is noteworthy that those found in the Kaiser criterion presented values higher than those simulated (parallel analysis) it was identified that the scale in question is unifatorial, because in the second factor (see table 5), the value observed in the Kaiser criterion was lower than the value in the parallel analysis.

Attentive to the interpretation of the factor item, two judges specialized (in statistics and psychological evaluation) in the analyses made, contributed with their judgment, corroborating the decision that was expected: the unifatoriality of the instrument.

Aware of these criteria, a Factorial Analysis of the Main Components (PC) was performed with oblique rotation, eigenvalue (own value) > 1.00 to define the factor and saturation of ±0.30 for retention of the items. The use of this technique was quite adequate through the following indicators: KMO = 0.79 and the Bartlett Sphericity Test, $\chi2/gl$ = 93.28/15, p< 0.001.

The extraction results revealed the presence of a single factor, according to what was found in the analysis for decision making - own values (eigenvalues) equal or higher than 1 (Kaiser Criterion), graphical distribution of own values (Cattell Criterion) and the parallel analysis; this factor, together, explained 37.33% of its construction variance.

To facilitate the reader's understanding, the content of each item, its saturation (factor load) and communality, as well as the indicators of internal consistency (Cronbach's alpha) and variance explained by the factor were presented. It can be observed that all these indicators were within the psychometric pattern required by the literature (Hair et al., 2005; Dancey & Reidy, 2006; Pasquali, 2011). As shown in Table 7 below:

Table 6 : Analysis of the main components (PC) of the debt attitude scale.

items	aif	h2
EAE 8.	0,83	0,70
EAE 2.	0,82	0,71
EAE 3.	0,76	0,59
EAE 4.	0,69	0,50
EAE 5.	0,63	0, 41
EAE 1.	0,62	0,38
Total number of items	06	
Own values	2,24	
Variance Explained	37,34	
Alpha de Chronbach (α)	0,77	

Note:aif1= items size force; Factorial Load; h^2 = Cumunity.

Considering these results, it is possible to highlight that the factorial organization of the EAE is distributed in a single factor, for which it is not only sustained in its factorial scores ($\geq$ 0.30), as well as, the alpha, revealing a consistency of this measure for the sample context surveyed.

5.5 ANALYSIS OF THE INTRA AND INTER-CORRELATIONSHIP BETWEEN AND THE CONSTRUCTS OF IMPULSIVITY OF BARRATT AND DICKMAN AND THEIR RELATIONSHIP TO THE ATTITUDE OF INDEBTEDNESS.

Based on the statistical analyses presented above, the main objective of this book (to verify the influence of impulsiveness on the attitude of indebtedness) was met; thus, a Pearson correlation analysis was carried out in order to evaluate which of the constructs and their respective dimensions are related to the attitude of indebtedness.

In table 8, specifically, you can observe that there was a positive relationship between Barrat's impulsivity (total score) and his Motor , Attention and Non Planning dimensions, as well as Dickman's impulsivity (total score) and the dysfunctional impulsivity dimension; attention is drawn to the non-significant relationship with the non-functional impulsivity.

Table 7 : Intra and inter-variable impulsivity scores

Buildings/ Dimensions	Impulsivity Barrat	Motor Impulsivity of Barrat	Impulsivity Attention from Barrat	Impulsivity Planning of Barrat	NoImpulsivity Dickman	Functional Impulsivity of Dickman	Dysfunctional Impulsivity of Dickman
Impulsivity Barrat (total score)	---						
Motor Impulsivity of Barrat	0,635**	---					
Impulsivity Attention from Barrat	0,696**	0,364**	---				
Impulsivity Planning of Barrat	0,647**	0,287**	0,425**	---			
Impulsivity Dickman (total score)	0,246*	0,243*	0,294*	0,323**	---		
Functional Impulsivity of Dickman	-0,047	-0,087	0,089	-0,013	0,579**	---	
Dysfunctional Impulsivity of Dickman	0,256**	0,258**	0,251*	0,273**	0,672**	0,262**	---

Note: * p < 0.05

In table 9, it is possible to observe the relationship between impulsivity constructs and the attitude of indebtedness; it is noted that Barrat's impulsivity (total score) and the motor dimension of it, positively related with the attitude of indebtedness

Table 8 : Correlation scores between impulsivity and debt attitude.

Buildings/ Impulsivity Dimensions	Attitude of indebtedness	
Impulsivity Barrat	0,21*	
Motor Impulsivity of Barrat	0,25*	
Impulsivity Attention from Barrat		-0,01
Impulsivity No Planning of Barrat	0,04	
Impulsivity Dickman	0,24*	
Functional Impulsivity of Dickman		-0,02
Dysfunctional Impulsivity of Dickman	0,27*	

Note: * $p < 0.05$

As additional data, the correlation between the specific variables on purchasing behavior and indebtedness attitude was verified; positive correlations were observed between parcelled purchasing behavior, purchases with income commitment and indebtedness attitude (respectively, $r = 0.36$, $r = 0.22$, $r = 0.35$, $p < 0.05$).

Attention is drawn to the existence of the intra-relationship between parcelled purchasing behavior and purchases with income commitment ($r = 0.43$). Thus, probably the subject with the highest score in installment purchases behavior will have a higher commitment to his monthly income.

Based on these correlations, a univariate ANOVA was carried out in order to evaluate the attitude of indebtedness according to impulsiveness. For this, a distribution of the variables in tertiles was carried out, through which they were divided into categorical levels (low, moderate and high). It was observed that only significant result in the Dickman impulsivity construction (considering unifatorial score), referring to the high impulsivity score [$F (2.112 = 2.76)$, $p < 0.01$].

Thus, it was decided to evaluate the influence of the specific factors of each impulsivity construction. Regarding Dickman impulsivity, both the functional and dysfunctional impulse dimension did not present significant results. Regarding Barrat's impulsivity dimensions (Motor, Not Planning and Attention), only impulsive attention showed significant results [F (2.112 = 3.44), $p < 0.05$]; a higher score in low attention was observed.

It was also decided to carry out a variable Anova on the behavior of installment purchases and purchases with the commitment of income due to the attitude of indebtedness. It was observed that in the attitude of indebtedness the highest scores were for the high commitment to similar purchases [F (2.112 = 9.73), $p < 0.01$] and the high commitment to monthly income [F (2.112 = 3.28), p < 0.01].

6 DISCUSSION OF RESULTS

This book aimed to evaluate the correlation between impulsiveness and attitude to indebtedness in subjects of the adult population in the city of Natal - RN. The intention to research this subject is due to the fact that the Brazilian population has found itself in a very large condition of indebtedness. According to Souza (2019), more than 59% of Brazilian families had some type of debt, a situation that not only interferes in purchasing behavior, but also in the emotional and interpersonal organization of those in debt.

Initially, it proposed the construction of a measure on indebtedness, since the only one that exists only seeks a more descriptive analysis focusing on a perspective of economic and sociodemographic behavior, but nothing very psychologically based. Thus, the supposed scale has shown itself to be both discriminated against in the distribution of its responses and representative of the correlated factor items. And in factorial analysis, it revealed psychometric indicators that guaranteed its unifatorial quality.

With this, he not only guaranteed a measure focused on the theory of attitudes, contemplating the phenomenon of indebtedness, but he also presented a measure that is capable of verifying the attitude of indebtedness, which focuses on the conative dimension of these attitudes.

In this sense, Ribeiro (2018) explains that the blame for the indebtedness may even be of an economic system that offers, without measures, credit with greater access, being disproportionate to the consumer's condition of consumption; but, also, it may be justified that the situation of the consumer's debt is of the debtor himself, due to his lack of "subjective" orientation (emotional or behavioral) in relation to the financial assets that are offered to him. In other words: he has no control over and is enchanted by the offer, with no projection that he will soon have to pay.

However, Acordi (2019) states that indebtedness does not only have its negative side. In certain situations, debts can bring benefits, because when they happen in a "controlled" way they promote a better quality of life for the individual. Indebtedness occurs in situations considered positive, not only as a need to purchase, but as an opportunity.

However, considering the findings in the research, the reflection exposed by Acordi (2019) is different from the findings in this study; both a motor impulsiveness (which is related to the non-inhibition of responses incoherent with the context) approached in the construct developed by Barrat, and the dysfunctional impulsiveness (refers to the tendency of a person to act with less prudence, placing them in social and behavioral difficulties) considered by Dickman, are influential in the attitude of indebtedness. Thus, being in debt is likely to be based on personality traits that are quite inconsistent with social consumer demand.

Thus, the person who values having a clean name, being a good payer, in the conception of Acordi (2019), may dysfunctionally be encouraged with ways to remedy the previous debt with new obligations, thus increasing the financial deficits; in fact, this author is right in stating this, because the personalistic dimensions of impulsiveness (motor and dysfunctional) in its different evaluation constructs (aimed at mental health) is a condition, *sine quo non*, to once again enter the process of indebtedness. Precisely because in impulsiveness there is no discipline, emphasizing a circular attitude of consumption.

Considering the reflection in the paragraph above, it is necessary to emphasize that impulsiveness is a psychological variable that is not so simple to be evaluated; because, according to Malloy-Diniz et al. (2010), it is a construct that contemplates a complex phenotype, which has characteristics in different cognitive and behavioral patterns, which can be observed in people's daily lives. Thus, a certain parsimony is necessary when considering these results, with exclusivity for a mental disorder, since impulse is approached in such definitions as a condition of behavioral problem.

After all, emphasizing an impulsive specificity as a disorder should not be a priority at the beginning of an evaluation; according to Evenden (1999; Moeller et al., 2001), not a few people who, at some point in life, presented an impulsive behavior or even say something without thinking about the causes, as well as not disregarding cultural differences, different stages of life, economic and political contexts.

In general, it is considered that the factors that lead to indebtedness are not few and can have the influence of areas of the personal life of the human being, of the intrinsic and extrinsic factors contemplated by psychological and sociological science. The fact of approaching such a theme, which, associated to the evaluation of the personality, concerns the development of a perspective that can unite clinical and social phenomena, contributing to better conduct contemporary emotional disorders.

The main concern of the research was to verify the impulsivity relationship and the indebtedness attitude. A second hypothesis was that those respondents with a higher impulsivity score had a higher indebtedness score. The results presented not only confirm what was expected, corroborating the conception of Abreu, Tavares and Cordás (2008; Siqueira et al., 2012), since, according to these authors, the impulse is one of the major generators of indebtedness.

Going back to table 8, it can be observed that when taking impulsiveness as a total score, either in Barrat's conception or in Dickman, both scales correlate positively with the attitude of indebtedness. Such results may be related to cognitive limitations or even dysfunctional beliefs of the indebted (cf. Malloy-Diniz et al., 2010; Vieira, 2014), because, based on the definitions of the impulsivity construct, in general, the two conceptions highlight difficulties in the control of decision making, elaboration and planning action, a condition which would contribute to the stimulus of consumption when the object is presented to such consumer.

Therefore, when considering this study we suggest a greater focus on cognitive factors associated with indebtedness. The perception, previous reflection and reasoning, for example, when insufficient lead the subject to impulsive purchases. On the contrary, when the subject is capable of self-perception, he or she is excluded as targets from the sales strategies developed especially to persuade these customers.

This affirmation corroborates what Vieira (2014) says, so that in situations where subjects are challenged concomitantly by the demand for cognitive activity and temptation, it is very likely that this individual will give in to the impulse of purchase.

The above-mentioned author also states that individuals who are in the habit of 'borrowing' have a low capacity to resist the response that first comes to mind, and show the exhaustion of necessary self-control. This fact, which may be associated with installment purchases and facilitated credit, since the possibilities of easy access to installment payments on the credit card lead the individual to buy in a disorderly manner, consecutively, if individual.

However, it attributes these results to a kind of correlational empiria, simply by using a quantitative methodology, it is known that one must recognize a reflexive limit in the explanations of this study.

It is also noticeable, when considering these findings, that impulsiveness of purchase is also related to a more subjective interpretation; it is possible to give rise to a conception in which consumption-indebtedness can be associated with a 'desire' to supply voids of an affective character and is associated with low self-esteem and affective deprivation.

The emotional, which in this sense is related to affective need, is therefore a state or condition that is considered an immediate reaction to a situation that is also considered favorable or unfavorable. When referring to immediacy, it is associated with condensation, and is therefore summarized in a pleasant or painful feeling, leading the individual to face the situation through the resources he possesses (Abbagnano, 1998).

The suggestions in the above paragraphs about the most subjective issue, in the results could be interpreted in the relation between Barrat's motor impulsivity, Dickman's general impulsivity and dysfunctional impulsivity, since they raise precisely this kind of logic (subjectivist) of the debt disorder. That is, because it does not have an emotional control, which may be associated with cognitive limits or even cognitive dissonance, the only way that the consumer would have to soften his internal conflict would be to buy; this attitude would associate the motor impulsivity (influencing the lack of inhibition of the incoherent responses that present themselves in the context), when in excess and out of control, the dysfunctional impulsivity, capable of leading the subject into debt (cf. Nolf, 1988; Powers, & Jack, 2013; Vilasanti, 2018).

In this conception of impulsiveness, as a psychological determinant, a factor of greater influence on indebtedness, it is also possible that there is a relationship with the symptoms of anxiety and depression, since to buy how much impulse (based on the affective or cognitive stimulus), is much more than a simple dissonance, since such symptoms, on the one hand, arouse action to correspond to what one wishes to be affirmed, on the other hand, in the case of depression, arouse action to get out of melancholic discomfort (cf. Artifon & Piva, 2013; Lucena et al, 2014; Souza, 2019).

7 FINAL CONSIDERATIONS

In general, the results of this study showed that the supposed measure on indebtedness revealed quite reliable indicators of psychometric quality, a condition that may suggest its use in future studies on indebtedness. Also, attention is drawn to the Barrat and Dickman impulsivity scale, which revealed consistency in the evaluation of people who indicated being in debt.

In view of the assumptions, it is suggested that indebtedness is related not only to financial education, but also to other factors of psychological organization. According to Vieira et al (2013), the perception and behavior of financial risk can also be considered a set of evaluation that contributes to explain indebtedness. Thus, it is not enough to educate economically, but it is necessary to educate emotionally the personnel destined to consumption.

Even considering that the results presented both revealed acceptable psychometric indicators as well as relationships among the variables proposed within the hypothetical pattern required, which, having achieved the intended objectives, it is believed that in future studies it could be useful to evaluate the relationship of the same variables associated with others relating to the dynamics and family system of consumption, as well as the perception of respondents regarding the consumption system proposed by the market; another variable, which suggests much impact, would be the evaluation of satisfaction with consumption and post-consumption guilt.

Finally, a promising context for future studies would be the comparison of those respondents with and without a diagnosis of the psychological disorder, especially those undergoing therapeutic and/or psychiatric treatment.

REFERENCES

Abbagnano, N. (1998). *Dictionary of philosophy.* São Paulo: Martins Fontes.

Abreu, C.N. , Tavares, H., & Cordás, T. A . (2008). *Clinical manual of impulse control disorders.* Artmed Editora.

I woke up, F. P. C. (2019). *Personal finances, family indebtedness and quality of life of the server.* Dissertation (Masters) - Universidade Tecnológica Federal do Paraná. Graduate Program in Public Administration in National Network, Curitiba.

Alvarez, Nelly Loyola. Validity *and Reliability of Barratt's Impulsivity Scale Version 11 (Bis-11) on Incarcerated Women.* Thesis (Bachelor's Degree in Psychology with a minor in Clinical Psychology). Faculty of Arts and Human Sciences. Lima-2011.

Amato, C. A. H., Brunoni, D., Boggio, P. S. (2018). *Developmental Disorders: Interdisciplinary Studies.* São Paulo: Memnon. Available at: https://www.mackenzie.br/fileadmin/ARQUIVOS/Public/6-pos-graduacao/upm-higienopolis/mestrado-doutorado/disturbios_desenvolvimento/2019/DISTU%CC%81RBIOS-DO-DESENVOLVIMENTO-eBOOK-1.pdf

American PsychiatricAssociation (2014). DSM-V: *Diagnostic and Statistical Manual of Mental Disorders* (5th Edition). Porto Alegre: Artmed.

Araújo, M. M., Malloy-Diniz, L. F. & Rocha, F L. (2009). *Impulsivity and traffic accident. Revista de Psiquiatria Clínica,* 36(2), 60-68.

Arce, E., &Santisteban, C. (2006). *Impulsivity: the review. Pscothema,* 18(2), 213-220.

Artifon, S., & Piva, M. (2013). *Indebtedness today: psychological factors involved in this process.* Available at: http://www.psicologia.pt/artigos/ver_artigo. php?codigo=A0771. Access in Oct. 2019.

Ávila-Batista, Ana Cristina; Marín Rueda, Fabián Javier. *Construction and Psychometric Studies of a Psycho-USF Impulsivity Assessment Scale,* v. 16, n. 3. pp. 285-295 Universidade São Francisco São Paulo, 2011.

Bahovec, V., Barbić, D., &Palić, I. (2015). Testing the effects of financial literacy on debt behavior of financial consumers using multivariate analysis methods. *Croatian Operational Research Review,*6, 361–371. doi:10.17535/crorr.2015.0028

Barratt, E. (1959). *Anxiety and Impulsiveness related to Psychomotor efficiency.* Perceptual and Motor Skill, 9, 191-198. DOI: 10.2466/PMS. 9.3.191-198

Barratt, E. S., & Patton, J. H. (1983). Impulsivity: Cognitive, behavioral, and psychophysiological correlates. In M. Zuckerman (Ed.), *Biological bases of sensation-seeking, impulsivity, and anxiety* (pp. 77–121). Hillsdale, NJ: Lawrence Erlbaum Associates.

Barratt, E.S. (1993). *Impulsivity: Integrating cognitive, behavioral, biological, and environmental data.* In W. G. McCown, J. L. Johnson, & M. B. Shure (Orgs.), The impulsive client: Theory, research, and treatment (pp. 39–56). Washington, DC, US: American Psychological Association.

Barratt, ES. *Anxiety and impulsiveness related to psychomotor efficiency.* Percept Mot Skills. 1959; 9(2): 191-8

Beck. A. T., &Alford, B. A. (2000). *The integrating power of cognitive therapy.* Porto Alegre: Artes médicassul.

Billieux, J. et al. (2008). *Are all facets of impulsivity related to self-reported compulsive buying behavior? Personalityand Individual Differences.* Disponível em: http://www.uclep.be/wp-content/uploads/pdf/Pub/Billieux_PAID_2008.pdf. Acesso em set. 2019.

Binotto, S., et al. The factors influencing consumer behavior: a study in an agricultural cooperative in RS. *RGC* - Vol. 01, N° 02, 2° Sem. 2014, Págs. 13-26.

Bonomo, B., &Mainardes, E. W. (2014). *Analysis of the Relationship Between Unplanned Purchases and Personal Indebtedness.* IXXXVIII ANPAD meeting, 1-13. Available at: http://www.anpad.org.br/admin/pdf/2014_EnANPAD_MKT425.pdf. Access in Oct. 2019.

Bonomo, B., Mainardes, E. W., &Laurett, R. (2017). Unplanned Purchasing and Personal Indebtedness: A Relationship Analysis. *Revista Administração em Diálogo,* 19(3), 49-69. Available at: http://www.spell.org.br/documentos/ver/46811/compra-nao-planejada-e-endividamento-pessoal--uma-analise-de-relacao-

Brandtner, M., & Serralta, F. B. (2016). Cognitive-Behavioral Therapy for Compulsive Shopping: A Systematic Case Study. *Psychology: Theory and Research*, 32 (1), 181-188. http://dx.doi.org/10.1590/0102-37722016012116181188. Access in Sep.2019.

Brito-Costa, S. Moisão, A; Briegas, J.J.M. Castro, F.V. *Portuguese version of the impulsivity scale EIB-11: psychometric properties.* Conf. Cephalal., et Neurol.,v..29, n.1, 11-17. Dalla Ricerca. 2019.

Brower, M. C., & Price, B. H. (2001). Neuropsychiatry of frontal lobe dysfunction in violent and criminal behaviour: a critical review. *Journal of neurology, neurosurgery, and psychiatry, 71*(6), 720–726. https://doi.org/10.1136/jnnp.71.6.720

Campara, J. P., Vieira, K. M., & Ceretta, P. S. (2016). Understanding Attitude to Indebtedness: Behavioral Factors and Socio-Economic Variables Determine It? *Revista Eletrônica de Ciência Administrativa*, 15(1), 5-24.

Caron, E., Lefèvre, F., & Lefèvre, A. M. C. (2015). After all, are we or are we not a consumer society? Health consequences. *Ciência & Saúde Coletiva, 20*(1*)*, 145-153. https://doi.org/10.1590/1413-81232014201.18812013

Caron, E; Lefèvre, F; Lefèvre, A.M.C. *After all, are we or are we not a consumer society? Health consequences.* Available at: http://www.scielo.br/pdf/csc/v20n1/pt_1413-8123-csc-20-01-00145.pdf Access in nov. 2019.

Claudino, L. P., Nunes, M. B., Oliveira, A. R., &Campos, O. V. (2009*). Financial education and indebtedness: a case study with public institution employees.* XVI Brazilian Congress of Costs, Vitória, ES. Available at: https://anaiscbc.emnuvens.com.br/anais/article/view/1029/1029.

Claes, L., Vertommen, H., & Braspenning, N. (2000). Psychometric properties of the Dickman Impulsivity Inventory. *Personality and Individual Differences, 29*(1), 27–35. https://doi.org/10.1016/S0191-8869(99)00172-5

Cloninger CR, Svrakic DM, Przybeck TR (1993) The Psychobi technological model of temperament and character. *Psychiatry Arc Gen*; 50: 975-989.

Cohen R. A., Rosenbaum A., Kane R. L., Warnken W. J., & Benjamin S. (1999) Neuropsychological correlates of domestic violence. Violence and Victims, 14(4), 397–411.

Costa, P. T., & McCrae, R. (1992). Normal personality evaluation in clinical practice: The NEO Personality Inventory. *Psychological evaluation.*

Costa, S. A. (2019). *Personal financial planning: a proposal for the inancial health of the Brazilian class C.* Fernando Pessoa University Porto - Portugal.

Dalgalarrondo P. (2008*). Psychopathology and semiology of mental disorders.* 2nd edition. Porto Alegre: Artemd. 2008.

Dancey, C. P., & Reidy, J. (2006). *Statistics without mathematics for psychology.* Porto Alegre: Artmed.

Dias, C. O., Arenas, N. C. S., Arenas, M. V. D., & Silva, R. M. P. (2017). Financial education profile of academics in the accounting, administration and economics courses of a Brazilian federal institution of higher education. *XVII International Colloquium on University Management.* University, development and future in the knowledge society. Available at: https://repositorio.ufsc.br/xmlui/bitstream/handle/123456789/181535/102_00105.pdf?sequence=1sAllowed=y

Dickman, S. J. (1990) Functional and dysfunctional impulsivity: personality and cognitive correlates. *Journal of Personality and Social Psychology,*58 (1),95-102.

Dickman, S. J. Impulsivity, arousal and attention. *Personality and Individual Differences,* 2000.

Dickman, S.J. & Meyer, D.E. (1988). Impulsivity And Speed-Accuracy Tradeoffs In Information Processing. *Journal Of Personality And Social Psychology, 54,* 274-290.

Donadio, R., Campanario, M. A., & Rangel, A. D. (2012). The role of financial literacy and credit card in the indebtedness of Brazilian consumers. *Revista Brasileira de Marketing,* 11 (1), 75-93.

Echeburúa, E., Bravo, R. M., & Aizpiri, J. (2008). Personality variables, psychopathological alterations and personality disorders in alcohol-dependent patients according to Cloninger's typology of alcohol abuse. *Psicothema, 20*(4), 525-3

Eric R, et al. (2005). Driving anger, sensation seeking, impulsiveness, and boredom proneness in prediction of unsafe driving. Accid Anal

Prev.37:341-
8   https://www.sciencedirect.com/science/article/abs/pii/S0001457
504000995?via%3Dihub#!

Evenden, J. L. (1999). Varieties of impulsivity. *Psychopharmacology, 146* (4), 348-61.

Eysenck, S. B., & Eysenck, H. J. (1977). The place of impulsiveness in a dimensional system of personality description. *British Journal of Social & Clinical Psychology, 16*(1), 57-68.

Eysenck, S. B., Pearson, P. R., Easting, G., & Allsopp, J. F. (1985). Age norms for impulsiveness, venturesomeness and empathy in adults. *Personality and Individual Differences,* 6(5), 613–619. https://doi.org/10.1016/0191-8869(85)90011-X

Faul F., Erdfelder E., & Buchner A., Lang A.-G. (2009). *Statistical power analyses using G*Power 3.1: tests for correlation and regression analyses.* Behavior Research Methods, 41, 1149-1160.

Fernandes, D. A. R. (2014). *Validation studies of the Barratt BIS-11 impulsivity scale for a sample of the Portuguese population.* Faculty of Psychology and Educational Sciences. UC/FPCE - University of Coimbra 2014.

Ferrari, A. T. et al. (2019). The influence of impulsive and procrastinating behaviour on financial decision making from the perspective of devaluation due to delay. *Perspectives in Management & Knowledge, 9 (1)*, 101-121.

Ferreira, S. S. C. (2013). *Exploration Motor Vs Impulsivity - Case study.* Instituto Superior Politécnico Gaya. Escola Superior de Educação de Santa Maria. Dissertation (Masters).

Figueira, R. F., Pereira, R. C. F. (2014). I must not negotiate, paid when I can: an analysis of the history of consumer indebtedness. *Revista Brasileira de Marketing.* DOI: 10,5585/remark. v13i5,2744

Flowers, S. A. M., Vieira, K. M., & Colonel, D. A. (2013). Influence of behavioral factors on the propensity to indebtedness. *Revista de Administração FACES Journal,* 12(2), 13-35.

Ant, N. S., Aguiar, M. & Omar, A. (2008). Search for antisocial and delitive sensations and conducts in young people. *Revista Psicologia: Ciência e Profissão, 28*(4), 668-681.

Formiga, N. S., Fleury, L. F. O., Fandiño, A. M., & Souza, M. A. (2016). Empirical evidence of a measure of organizational anomie in Brazilian workers. *Revista de Psicologia da UCV*, *18*(1), 43-59. DOI 10.18050/revpsi.v18n1a4.2016

Ant, N. S.; Omar, A. G., & Aguiar, M. (2010). Search for sensation and potential use of drugs in college students. *Psicologia Revista*, 19(1), 97-118.

France, D.B. (2019). *An analysis of spending and the propensity to indebtedness in relation to commemorative and thematic dates.* Federal University of Paraíba. João Pessoa, PB.

Galvão, M. C.; Almeida, A. N. *The pattern of family consumption and behavior by gender in Brazil: an analysis using the family budget survey.* 2008/2009. Available at: http://repositorio.ipea.gov.br/bitstream/11058/8500/1/ppp_n50_padr %C3%A3o.pdf. Access in Nov. 2019.

Gao, Y., Chen, H., Jia, H., Ming, Q., Yi, J., & Yao, S. (2016). Dysfunctional feedback processing in adolescent males with conduct disorder. *International Journal of Psychophysiology, 99,* 1–9. https://doi.org/10.1016/j.ijpsycho.2015.11.015

Garcia, M. S. (2018). *Adaptation of the UPPS-P scale and its applicability in the Brazilian population (manuscript).* Belo Horizonte.

Gattás, I.G. (2014). Attention deficit/hyperactivity disorder. In Coêlho, B. M., Pereira, J. G., Assumpção, T. M., & Santana Jr., G. L. (Orgs.), Psiquiatria *da Infância e da Adolescência (pp.* 277-306). New Hamburg: Sinopsys.

Giareta, L. F. (2011). Consumer behavior in the purchasing decision process. III Unisalesian Scientific Meeting and Education Symposium. *Education and Research: the production of knowledge and the training of researchers.* Lins, 17 - 21 October 2011.

Gomes, A. K. V. (2016). Translation, cross-cultural adaptation and factorial structure of the *Brazilian version of Dickman's impulsivity inventory.* Dissertation (Master's Degree) Universidade Federal de Viçosa.

Gomes, Á. K. V. Diniz, L. F. M. Lage, G. M. , Miranda, D. M., Paula, J. J., Costa, D., & Albuquerque, M. R. (2017). *Translation, adaptation and validation of the Brazilian version of Dickman Impulsivity Inventory (Br-DII). Frontiers in Psychology, 8,* Article ID 1992.

Grando, A. P. , & Magro, M. P. D. *"Consumption, therefore I exist": the senses of consumption in the solidarity economy.* 2011. Available at:

http://pepsic.bvsalud.org/scielo. php?script=sci_arttext&pid=S1809-52672011000200002. Access in nov. 2019.

Guerra, D. de S. , Peñaloza, V. , Quezado, I., & Araújo, M. (2016). *Analysis of the Relations between Impulsive and Compulsive Purchasing Personality Traits.* 12th Latin American Congress on Retail and Consumerism: Digital Transformation in Retail.

Gutierrez, B. P. B. (2004). Determinantes of planned and Impulse buying: the case of the philippiness. *Asia Pacific Management Review*, 9(6), 1061-1078. Disponível em: https://pdfs.semanticscholar.org/9f2b/ef3b4eb3404311ce625c63897 6ce7da0543c.pdf.

Hair, J., Anderson, R., Tatham, R. and Black, W. (2008) *Multivariate Data Analysis.* McGraw Hill Publishing, Boston.

Hanna, H. S.; Todorov, J. C. (2020). Self-Control Models in Experimental Behavior Analysis: Utility and Criticism. *Psychology: theory and research*, 18 (3), 337-343.

Hennigen, I. (2012). *The reverse side of the consumer-credit system: (super) consumer debt.* VI Encontro Nacional de Estudos do Consumo, II Encontro Luso brasileiro de Estudos do Consumo. Available at: http://docplayer.com.br/52886335-O-lado-avesso-do-sistema-consumo-credito-super-endividamento-do-consumidor.html.

Hoaken, P. N. S., Shaughnessy, V. K., & Pihl, R. O. (2003). Executive cognitive functioning and aggression: Is it an issue of impulsivity? *Aggressive Behavior, 29*(1), 15–30. https://doi.org/10.1002/ab.10023.

Hutz, C.S, Bandeira, D. R., & Trentini, C. M. (2015). *Psychometry. Psychological Evaluation*. Artmed Editora.

Jobim, S. S. A., & Losekann, V. L. (2015). *Financial literacy: measurement of the behavior and financial knowledge of university students of the campaign region, Rio Grande do Sul. Social and Human*, Santa Maria, 28(2), 125 - 139. DOI: 10.5902/ 23175818835.

Lake, F. W. G., & Kings, J. M. O. (2016). Consumer society in Bauman and Drummond's view: interdiscursiveness in the authors' works. *Portal of Electronic Journals of UFMA. São Luís/MA, 6* (12), 39-50. Available at: < http://www.periodicoseletronicos.ufma.br/index.php/bauman/article/v iew/6225/4293>. Access on: November 15, 2018.

Lea, S. E. G., Webley, P., & Levine, R. M. (1993). The economic psychology of consumer debt. *Journal of Economic Psychology, 14*(1), 85-119. https://doi.org/10.1016/0167-4870(93)90041-I.

Lima, L.G. (2016). *Personal Finances: a study on the effective civil servants of the City Hall of São Fernando-RN.* Caicó, RN: UFRN.

Littwin, A. K. (2008). Beyond Usury: A Study of Credit Card Use and Preference Among

Low-Income Consumers. *Texas Law Review*, 56, 451-506.

Loo, R. (1978). Individual difference and the perception of traffic signs. Human Factors, NO. 20. Pp. 65-74.

Lopes, A. V., Badio, C. A., Coimbra, J. C. M., Pozzan, L., & Biazoto, R. P. (2014). *Financial literacy of students the courses of business administration, economics and accounting sciences of FECAP.* HIGH SCHOOL, 4(5), 53-71.

Lucena, W. G. L. (2014). *Factors influencing indebtedness and default in the real estate sector in the city of Toritama-PE in light of behavioral finance.* HOLOS, 30 (6). DOI: https://doi.org/10.15628/holos.2014.1084.

Luengo, M. A., Carrillo-de-la-Peña, M. T., & Otero, J. M. (1991). The components of impulsiveness: A comparison of the I.7 Impulsiveness Questionnaire and the Barratt Impulsiveness Scale. *Personality and Individual Differences, 12*(7), 657–667. https://doi.org/10.1016/0191-8869(91)90220-6.

Macdonald, Scott & Erickson, Patricia & Wells, S & Hathaway, A & Pakula, Basia. (2008). Predicting violence among cocaine, cannabis, and alcohol treatment clients. Addictive behaviors. 33. 201-5. 10.1016/j.addbeh.2007.07.002.

Malloy-Diniz, L. F. *Translation and cultural adaptation of Barratt Impulsiveness Scale (BIS-11) for application in Brazilian adults.* (2010). Available at: http://www.scielo.br/pdf/jbpsiq/v59n2/a04v59n2.pdf. Access in October 2019.

Malloy-Diniz, L. F., Neves, F. S., Abrantes, S. S. C., Fuentes, D., & Corrêa, H. (2009). Suicide behavior and neuropsychological assessment of type I bipolar patients. *Journal of affective disorders, 112*(1-3), 231-236.

Malloy-Diniz, L., Fuentes, D., Borges Leite, W., Correa, H., & Bechara, A. (2007). Impulsive behavior in adults with attention deficit/hyperactivity disorder: characterization of attentional, motor and cognitive impulsiveness. *Journal of the International Neuropsychological Society, 13*, 693–698

Marques, M. L. M. & Frade, C. (2003). *Regulating over-indebtedness* (Research Report). Coimbra, Portugal, Centre for Social Studies, Faculty of Economics, University of Coimbra.

Marchesini Junior, A. (2012). The selling life model of the "consumer society" - DOI 10,5216/ag.v6i2,16270. *Ateliê Geográfico, 6*(2), 131-147. https://doi.org/10.5216/ag.v6i2.16270.

Matioli, Matheus Rozário, Rovani, Érica Aparecida, & Noce, Mariana Araújo. (2014). The borderline personality disorder from the viewpoint of psychologists with training in Psychoanalysis. *Health & Social Transformation, 5(1),* 50-57. Recovered in 25 of feveiro de 2020, from http://pepsic.bvsalud.org/scielo.php?script=sci_arttextid=S2178-70852014000100009ng=ptlng=pt.

Meira, C. H. M. G. & Nunes, M. L. T. (2005). *Clinical psychology, psychotherapy and the student of psychology.* Paidéia, 15(32), 339-343. http://www.scielo.br/pdf/paideia/v15n32/03.pdf.

Miles, J. N. V., & Shevlin, M. E. (2001). *Applying regression and correlation: A guide for students and researchers.* London: Sage Publications.

Moeller, F. G. et al. (2001). Psychiatric aspects of impulsivity. *The American Journal of Psychiatry, 158* (11), 1783-1793.

Moeller, F. G., Barratt, E. S., Dougherty, D. M., Schmitz, J. M., & Swann, A. C. (2001). Psychiatric aspects of impulsivity. *American JournalPsychiatry*, 158, 1789-1793.

Mitchell, S.H. (1999). Measures of impulsivity in cigarette smokers and nonsmokers.Psychopharmacology, 146 (4), 455-464.

Moraes, P. H. P. (2011). *Relationship between impulsivity and suicide in a patient with bipolar affective disorder.* MSc Dissertation, Instituto de Ciências Biológicas, Universidade Federal de Minas Gerais, Belo Horizonte, Brazil.

Morals Son, E. (2019). *Law of minimum wage.* Available in: Access at http://www.fgv.br/cpdoc/acervo/dicionarios/verbete-tematico/lei-do-salario-minimo. Access in November 2019.

Neves, A. O. (2013). *Impulsivity, perception of parental educational practices, antisocial behavior and delinquents in adolescents: A sample in school context.* Dissertation (Masters), Instituto Supeior de Ciências da Saúde Egas Moniz. Monte de Caparica, Almada, Portugal.

Nolf, M. M. R. (1988). *Aspects of dissonance in purchasing behavior.* Dissertation. (Master's Degree) - Fundação Getúlio Vargas, São Paulo. Available at: http://bibliotecadigital.fgv.br/dspace/handle/10438/11559.

Otto, F. B., Willhelm, A. R., Almeida, R. M. M. (2016). Impulsivity in adolescence: relationship between impulsive behavior and performance in an intelligence test. *Psycho-pedagogy On Line , 1*, 10-22.

Otto, F. B. (2016). *Evaluation of impulsiveness in relation to performance in an intelligence test in adolescents.* Federal University of Rio Grande do Sul Institute of Psychology Graduate Program in Psychology. Porto Alegre.

Pacheco, G., Campara, J., & Costa Jr., N. (2018). Personality traits, attitude to indebtedness and financial knowledge: a portrait of the servants of the Federal University of Santa Catarina. *Revista de Ciências da Administração, 20*(52), 54-73. doi:https://doi.org/10.5007/2175-8077.2018V20n52p54.

Parcias, S.R., Sombrio, L.S., Flügel, N.T., Rosário, M.J., Souza, M.D., & Guimarães, A.C. (2015). Impulsive behavior: Study in a population of university students. *Revista de Atenção a Saúde, 12* (42), 36-41.

Pasquali, L. (2011). *Psychometry: test theory in psychology and education* (4th ed.). Petrópolis/RJ: Voices.

Patton J. H., Stanford M. S., & Barratt E. S. (1995). Factor structure of the Barratti mpulsiveness scale. *JournalClinical Psychological, 51*(6), 768-74. Disponível em: https://onlinelibrary. wiley.com/doi/abs/10.1002/1097-4679%28199511%2951%3A6%3C768%3A%3AAID-JCLP2270510607%3E3.0.CO%3B2-1?sid=nlm%3Apubmed. Acesso em novembro de 2019.

Pechorro, P., Oliveira, J. P., Gonçalves, R., & Jesus, S. (2018). Psychometric properties of a reduced version of Barratt's Impulsivity Scale - 11 in a school sample of Portuguese adolescents. *Revista Iberoamericana de Diagnóstico y Evaluación, 47*, 157-170. doi:10.21865/RIDEP47.2.11.

PEIC - National Consumer Debt and Default Survey. (2017). *Peic Analysis.* Available at: http://cnc.org.br/central-doconhecimento/pesquisas/economia/pesquisa-nacional-de-endividamento-e-inadimplencia-do-- 33.

Podsakoff, P. M., Scott B. M. & Podsakoff, N. P. (2003). Common method biases in behavioral research: A critical review of the literature and recommended remedies. *Journal of Applied Psychology.* 88 (5), p.879–903.

Polon, L.C.K. *Consumer society or the consumption of society? A confusingly perceived world.* (2011). Available at: http://cac-php.unioeste.br/projetos/gpps/midia/seminario6/arqs/Trab_completo s_economia_sociedade/Sociedade_de_consumo_ou_consumo_soc iedade.pdf. Access in December 2019.

Bridges, H. N. S. A., Ayres, L. C. N., Neto, O. S. S., &Silva, V. A. L. M S. (2014). *Financial Balance between Public Servants and Service Providers in João Pessoa.* Available at: http://cef.fgv.br/sites/cef. fgv.br/files/24_finance_balance_between_public_servers_and_provi ders_in_joao_person.pdf.

G1 Portal. The number of defaulters reaches 61.8 million and breaks a record, says Serasa. Available at: https://g1.globo.com/economia/noticia/2018/07/19/numero-de-inadimplentes-chega-a-618-milhoes-e-bate-recorde-diz-serasa.ghtml. Access in November 2019.

Potrich, A. C. G., Vieira, K. M. & Kirch, G. (2015). Determinants of Financial Literacy: Influence Analysis of Socio-economic and Demographic Variables. *R. Cont. Fin.* - USP, São Paulo, v. 26, n. 69, p. 362-377. DOI: 10.1590/1808-057x201501040.

Potrich, A. C. G., Vieira, K. M., & Kirch, G. (2014). Are you financially literate? Find out on the financial literacy thermometer. *Proceedings of the Brazilian Meeting on Behavioral Economics and Finance,* São Paulo, SP, Brazil.

Powers, T. L., & Jack, E. P. (2013). The influence of cognitive dissonance on retail product returns. *Psychology & marketing, 30* (8), 724-735.

Ribeiro, R.F. *The indebtedness of the working class in Brazil in the years 2000.* 2018. 249 p.

Ribeiro, S. P. (2016). CBT and executive functions in children with ADHD. *Revista Brasileira de Terapias Cognitivas, 12*(2), 126-134. https://dx.doi.org/10.5935/1808-5687.20160019.

Rizzotto, A. B., Guareschi, A. Zilli, J. B., &Tartas, R. L. (2016). *Determinants of Indebtedness: A Study for Step-Fund Women.* Available at: http://www.pucrs.br/face/wp-content/uploads/sites/6/2016/03/1_ALESSANDRA-BIAVATI-RIZZOTTO.pdf.

Rocha, N. Q. (2013). *The personality theory in Aron Beck's cognitive therapy. Dissertation to the graduate program in psychology at the Federal University of Juiz de Fora.* Available at: http://www.ufjf.br/ppgpsicologia/files/2010/01/Natalia-Quintela-Rocha.pdf.

Saleh, M. A. E. (2012). *An Investigation of the Relationship between Unplanned Buying and Post-purchase Regret. International Journal of Marketing Studies,* 4(4), p. 106-130. Disponível em: https://fac.ksu.edu.sa/sites/default/files/post-purchase_regret.pdf

Salgado, João Vinicius, Malloy-Diniz, Leandro Fernandes, Campos, Valdir Ribeiro, Abrantes, Suzana Silva Costa, Fuentes, Daniel, Bechara, Antoine, & Correa, Humberto. (2009). Neuropsychological assessment of impulsive behavior in abstinent alcohol-dependent subjects. *Brazilian Journal of Psychiatry,* 31(1), 4-9. https://doi.org/10.1590/S1516-44462009000100003.

Sediyama, C. Y. N. (2014). Investigation of the psychometric characteristics of the UPPS Impulsive Behavior Scale for a Brazilian population.

Silva, C. G., Santos, T. A., Costa, C. G., &Moreira, J. A. P. (2016). *The influence of financial education: an analysis of the financial decisions of academics in the course of accounting sciences in public higher education institutions in Paraíba.* III CONEDU national congress of education. Available at: http://www.editorarealize.com.br/revistas/conedu/trabalhos/TRABAL HO_EV056_MD1_SA8_ID9434_10082016205025.pdf.

Silveira, C., Norton, A., Brandão, I, & Roma-Torres, A. (2011). *Mental health in higher education students: Experience of the psychiatric consultation at Centro Hospitalar São João.* Acta Médica Portuguesa, 24(2), 247-256.

Siqueira, L. D., Castro, A. D. M., Caravalho, J., &Farina, M. C. (2012). The impulsiveness in internet shopping. *Revista Eletrônica de Estratégica de Negócios,* 5(1), 253-279.

Souza, G. S. *Indebtedness: seeking behavioral motivations and impacts on health. Dissertation (master's degree)* - Universidade Federal de Uberlândia, Graduate Program in Administration. (2019).

SPC BRAZIL. (2015). Increasingly *restricted credit makes default slow to 1.81% in February, says SPC Brasil.* Available at: http://www.aciv.com.br/noticias/credito-cada-vez-mais-restrito-faz-inadimplencia-desacelerar-para-181-em-fevereiro-diz-spc-brasil/.

Spósito, M.E.B. Capitalismo e Urbanização. *Context,* São Paulo, 2000, 10th edition.

Tabachnick, B. G., Fidell, L. S. *Using Multivariate Statistics.* 4 ed. Boston : Allyn and Bacon, 2001.

Struber D., Luck M., Roth G. (2008). Sex, aggression and impulse control: An integrative account. Neurocase, 14(1), 93–121. doi:10.1080/13554790801992743.

Tavares, H. (2008). Impulse control disorders: the return of Esquirol's instinctive monomania. *Revista Brasileira de Psiquiatria,* 30(Suppl. 1), Available at: https://dx.doi.org/10.1590/S1516-44462008000500001.

Teixeira, V. P. G. (2014). *Changes in executive functions, impulsiveness and aggressiveness in individuals dependent on crack.* Dissertation (Masters). Federal University of Alagoas.

Trigueiro, E. S. O. (2015). School Psychology and the Psychology student: elements for debate. *Revista Quadrimestral da Associação Brasileira de Psicologia Escolar* e Educacional, 19(2), 223-231. http://dx.doi.org/10. 1590/2175-3539/2015/0192820.

Vasconcelos, A.G. (2012). *Cultural adaptation and investigation of the psychometric properties of Barratt Impulsiveness Scale (BIS-11).* PhD Thesis. Federal University of Minas Gerais. Belo Horizonte, MG.

Vasconcelos, AG, Sergeant, J, Corrêa, H., Mattos, P., & Malloy-Diniz, L. (2014). When self-reporting diverges from performance: The use of BIS-11 along with neuropsychological testing. *Psychiatry Research, 218 (*1-2), 236-243.

Velvet of Slope, T. M., Ikeda, A. A., &Santos, R. C. (2004). *Compulsive purchasing and the influence of the credit card.* RAE, 44(3), 89-99.

Vieira, C. P. *Cognitive Reflex and Indebtedness:* A Behavioral Analysis. Centro Sócio Econômico Departamento de Ciências Econômicas e Relações Internacionais. Federal University of Santa Catarina - UFSC. Florianópolis, 2014.

Vieira, K.M., Flores, S.A. M., Potrich, A. C., Campara, J. P., & Paraboni, A. L. (2013). Perception and financial risk behavior: analysis of the influence of occupation and other socio-demographic variables. *Revista de Gestão, Finanças e Contabilidade, 3* (3), Available at: http://www.atena.org.br/revista/ojs-2.2.3-06/index.php/RGFC/article/view/2170.

Vilasanti, V. (2018). Cognitive dissonance in consumer behavior research: a systematic study. *Revista De AdministraçãO Do Unisal, 8*(13). Retrieved from http://www.revista.unisal.br/sj/index.php/RevAdministracao/article/view/711

Whiteside S.P., Lynam D.R. *The Five Factor Model and impulsivity:* Using a structural model of personality to understand impulsivity. Personal. Individ. Differ. 2001.

Zancanaro, V. (2015). *Credit supply and default in Brazil.* Article presented to the Finance and Capital Markets Lato Sensu Post-Graduation Course, of the Administrative, Accounting, Economic and Communication Sciences Department (Dacec), of the Northwest Regional University of the State of Rio Grande do Sul (Unijuí) Available at: http://bibliodigital.unijui.edu.br:8080/xmlui/bitstream/handle/1234567 89/3923/Vin%C3%ADcius%20Zancanaro.pdf?sequence=1. Access in November 2019.

Zanirato, S. H. Rotondaro, T. Consumo, Um Dos Dilemas Da Sustentabilidade. Available at: http://www.scielo.br/scielo. php?script=sci_arttext&pid=S0103-40142016000300077. Estud. Advanced. v, 3. n. 88 São Paul. Sept. Dec. 2016.

Printed by Books on Demand GmbH, Norderstedt / Germany